POWER
·OVER·
PANIC

To Dr Eli Rafalowicz

'We paced along the lonely plain, as one who returns to his lost road, and till he reaches it, seems to go in vain.'

Dante, 'Purgatorio' in The Divine Comedy

2ND EDITION

POWER
·OVER·
PANIC

Freedom from Panic / Anxiety Related Disorders

BRONWYN FOX

Foreword by Garry McDonald

Prentice
Hall

Pearson Education Australia
Unit 4, Level 2
14 Aquatic Drive
Frenchs Forest NSW 2086

www.pearsoned.com.au

Publisher: Nella Soeterboek
Managing Editor: Susan Lewis
Cover and text design: Liz Nicholson, design BITE
Typesetting by The Type Group

Printed in Australia

2 3 4 5 05 04 03 02 01

National Library of Australia
Cataloguing-in-Publication Data

Fox, Bronwyn.
    Power over panic: freedom from panic/anxiety related
disorders.

    2nd ed.
    Bibliography.
    ISBN 1 74009 487 5.

    1. Anxiety - Popular works. 2. Panic attacks - Popular works.
    3. Panic disorders - Popular works. 4. Stress management. I. Title.

    616.85223

616.85223
FOX

Prentice Hall is an imprint of Pearson Education Australia.

CONTENTS

PART 1

Anxiety disorders and their effects   1

PART 2

Five steps to freedom and power   55

FOREWORD

BY GARRY McDONALD

As far as I am concerned, Bronwyn Fox gave me back my life. I was struggling to overcome a very public nervous breakdown in 1994 when I received a request from Bronwyn to speak at an inaugural dinner for a fledgling anxiety disorders organisation.

I get some pretty strange requests but I couldn't understand where this one had come from. Anxiety disorder? What the hell is an anxiety disorder, and why is this woman approaching me?

She had enclosed a copy of an earlier book of hers on anxiety and panic attacks. I had received a lot of pamphlets and advice from total strangers after my breakdown. They were mostly either Christian fundamentalist or new age and went straight into the recycling bin. But this book was a revelation. This was me.

I recognised myself immediately. I can't tell you the relief I felt when I realised what was wrong with me. It had a name and it was treatable! Until then I had seen various therapists and not one of them had actually said to me 'You have an anxiety disorder'.

One therapist told me my problem of fear would be more manageable if I worked only with people I trusted. Great! My self-confidence is just about zero and this guy's encouraging me to become completely helpless. And this from a clinical psychologist.

Another psychologist tried waving a pen in front of my eyes. When that didn't work she told me to wear a rubber band around my wrist and whenever I felt negative I was to snap the rubber band against my wrist. While I was reacting to the pain I was to replace the negative thought with a positive one. Well, my tolerance to pain must be greater than I imagined because it didn't have any effect, except for a slight tingling in my fingertips if I wore the rubber band for any length of time. How I was to manage any gangrene that developed she didn't say.

When the fear started to paralyse me again, my shrink put me on a drug that had a rather unpleasant side effect—it made me disinhibited.

Not a great quality for someone with social phobia. I would say or do the most inappropriate things at the most inappropriate times and usually to people I really cared about. I was getting quite desperate. And it was costing me a fortune.

When we eventually met, I quizzed Bronwyn on where I could get help. She pointed me in the right direction. Eight sessions later I was back on my feet.

Cognitive therapy is deceptively simple. It's the commitment and repetition that makes it work. And then one day the penny drops and you realise you now perceive things differently. You don't immediately jump to an irrational conclusion. I still use these skills to this day. Whenever I feel even the smallest amount of fear creeping up I nip it in the bud.

In this book Bronwyn explains very simply how to get your life back on track without drugs—just mind work and meditation. Meditation has a tremendous effect on the nervous system. I meditate twice daily and any stress just evaporates after twenty minutes. This quiet time really allows you to appreciate yourself just as you are. It gives you a stronger sense of self, and strong self-esteem is what good mental health is all about.

Bronwyn suffered from panic disorder for a number of years before devising this program. She is an inspiring teacher and a tireless crusader for the recognition of anxiety disorders which are a major problem within the community. She has heaps and heaps of wisdom which she shares with all. Make the most of this book. It will change your life.

Garry McDonald

INTRODUCTION

I experienced my first panic attack in October 1980 and it was downhill from that point on until mid 1984. Like all of us, my idea of recovery was intangible. All I wanted was to wake up one morning and find the disorder had gone. Finished. Over. Disappeared into the land of nightmares, never to return.

I had little idea of how to help myself, let alone how to recover. I learned to meditate in January 1981 in an effort to relax, but it wasn't until 1982 that I began to meditate on a regular basis. I had no concept of the underlying principles of meditation. All I knew in the beginning was that meditation enabled me to 'escape' during the day from my ongoing panic attacks and anxiety. But meditation is not an escape. If anything, it is the complete opposite. What I did not realise at the time was that meditation is in fact the oldest cognitive technique in the world.

Meditation became my teacher. Through my daily practice I became aware of how much of my ongoing distress was being created by the way I was thinking. I knew my thoughts were racing, panicking, anxious and negative. We all know this, but I came to understand how my thoughts actually created many of my symptoms and my ongoing distress. Seeing this connection with such clarity was the key. From it, I began to lose the fear of my experience because I could see how and why I was so anxious and why I was panicking. I also saw very clearly that I did in fact have a choice in what I thought about.

I began to adapt my meditation technique so that I could use its cognitive skills in everyday life. I also drew on the other skills inherent within the practice of meditation as I worked my way through my attacks, fears, anxiety, agoraphobia and a prescribed-drug addiction.

For me, recovery was a change of perception. I learnt to see my attacks and anxiety in another way. I saw them for what they were.

Although the attacks could feel very violent, I understood why they would not hurt me and I also came to understand why my anxiety would not hurt me.

Now, if I am overtired or sufficiently stressed, I may on occasion still have a spontaneous attack. As I am no longer frightened of them, I see them more as simply acknowledging that I am tired or overstressed and that I need to do something about it. As I am not afraid of them, they last for about thirty seconds and there is no residual fear or anxiety. What's thirty seconds every twelve months or so? It is nothing. When I had panic disorder, I could experience a number of attacks a day, some lasting for an hour or more. When I wasn't having an attack I would be extremely anxious about having another one and the cycle kept feeding on itself. I much prefer an occasional 30-second attack than a lifetime of panic and anxiety!

For me, the secret of recovery was the loss of fear of my panic attacks, anxiety and their associated fears. Lose the fear and we lose the anxiety and the disorder. Lose the fear and, if we do have an attack in the future, we prevent any escalation back into panic disorder.

I know and understand that people don't ever want to have another attack. We all want our recovery to mean no more attacks and no more anxiety. In fact, some of the treatments available set the recovery 'goalposts' to mean no more attacks at all. In my own experience, and my experience in working with other people with panic disorder, this is unrealistic. It is also in direct contradiction with the genetic contribution associated with panic disorder.

I was fortunate in finding a way to recover. Most of the people I see with an anxiety disorder have never been given the opportunity to learn to manage the disorder themselves. Yet the tens of thousands of people I have met with an anxiety disorder want to be able to do this.

Cognitive behavioural therapy (CBT) is now a 'best practice' in the treatment of anxiety disorders, but very few people are offered it as a treatment option. Even if they are offered CBT, there are very few resources available to meet the overwhelming demand in the community.

Anxiety disorders represent the largest mental health problem in Australia. It is ironic in this era of 'mutual obligation' that people with an anxiety disorder are denied the opportunity to help themselves by the very health services that treat them. It is not as if providing these services would increase health costs. In fact, it would save significant monies, not just within health budgets but also with disability and unemployment benefits and other associated costs. It would also increase productivity and reduce absentee rates within corporate Australia, not to mention workers' compensation claims.

In the United States the economic burden of anxiety disorders is estimated to be about US$42.3 billion in 1990 dollar terms ($1542 per sufferer) or US$63.1 billion in 1998 dollars (Greenberg et al. 1999). No Australian figures are available, but I have no reason to doubt that the Australian 'per sufferer' figure would be the equivalent of the American one.

It is not as if these costs are not recognised in Australia. As one government review noted: 'The opportunities for benefit to clients and their families and to the medium to longer term costs to the health system are potentially great if services were improved' (SAHC 1998).

These costs could be further reduced by early intervention strategies to minimise or prevent the development of anxiety disorders, yet resources for these are almost non-existent.

Since beginning to work in the area of anxiety disorders I have seen many changes over the years. There is now greater awareness and understanding of anxiety disorders and many people are being diagnosed on first presentation to their doctor. But the one area that has not improved is the provision of services for people with anxiety disorders. Until this is addressed, people will continue to suffer unnecessarily and the costs to taxpayers and corporate Australia will continue to increase.

Bronwyn Fox
March 2001

ACKNOWLEDGEMENTS

The case histories in this book are true although the names have been changed to ensure privacy for the individual concerned. I express my appreciation and thanks to the many people who, like myself, have had or now have panic disorder/agoraphobia for sharing their histories with me. Not only have you increased my own understanding of the disorder, you have also taught me much about myself.

Specific thanks to Carol Barker, Jasmin Arthur-Jones, Anthony Byrne and the Committee of the Panic Anxiety Disorder Association Inc. My thanks also to Christopher Edwards, Clinical Psychologist, Associate Professor Julian Hafner and Professor Larry Evans for their help, friendship, support and encouragement.

FURTHER INFORMATION

For further information and contact details of your local anxiety disorders association, visit the Panic Anxiety Hub's website:

http://www.panicattacks.com.au

or write to

Panic Anxiety Hub
PO Box 516
Goolwa, South Australia 5214

Bronwyn's workshop videos and a double cassette featuring a meditation tape designed for people with an anxiety disorder is available from the Panic Anxiety Hub.

PART 1
ANXIETY
DISORDERS
·AND THEIR·
EFFECTS

CHAPTER 1

EARLY INTERVENTION/ PREVENTION

Have you just begun to experience panic attacks? Are you becoming extremely anxious for what appears to be no reason? Has your doctor confirmed you are experiencing panic attacks or anxiety or both?

It is important you do not self-diagnose. This needs to be done by your doctor. Panic attacks and anxiety can mimic a number of physical conditions. You need your doctor's assessment to confirm that your symptoms are those of panic and anxiety. Once you have been diagnosed, you are in a position to be able to minimise or prevent any potential development of an anxiety disorder.

Like all of us who have experienced panic attacks and anxiety, you will be feeling quite frightened and confused. You will have heard people talk of having panic attacks, perhaps in the media or a family member or friend may have told you of their experience. However, hearing about them is one thing—actually having a panic attack or experiencing extreme anxiety, or both, is another! The words 'panic attack' and 'anxiety' don't really convey the ferocity of the experience. So when it happens to you, there doesn't seem to be any correlation between your understanding of the meaning of these words and your actual experience.

You will be wondering what is happening to you and why. You will be trying 'to pull yourself together'. You may be trying to 'think positive' but your efforts are only partially effective or perhaps not effective at all. You may have begun to search the Internet for information to help you understand your experience. You may have been reading bulletin boards or participated in chat rooms to speak with other people with similar experiences. While this may have provided some degree of reassurance, you could also be even more frightened by what you have learned.

You may have found that some people live with an anxiety disorder for years and that many struggle with the secondary effects of their disorder including agoraphobia, depression, perhaps a prescribed-drug addiction or alcohol dependency. You may even have been told by your doctor that you will just have to learn to live with it and/or you will be on medication for the rest of your life.

What you may not have learned is that people no longer need to 'learn to live with it'. In the past there were very few effective treatment options. Now there are several. Anxiety disorders were only recognised in 1980. And only since the mid 1990s are people being correctly diagnosed within a reasonable time frame. However, early diagnosis does not necessarily mean that people are being offered effective treatment strategies such as cognitive behavioural therapy.

It is the lack of an immediate diagnosis and/or effective treatment strategies that leads to the development of an anxiety disorder and the secondary conditions associated with it. It may also be the reason why many people are told by their doctors to learn to live with it, because their doctors have not seen people recover in the long term.

Much of the suffering that appears to be inherent in anxiety disorders is actually preventable. Most people who have had panic disorder will say that, if they had been diagnosed in the beginning, had understood from the beginning, had known how to manage their panic attacks from the beginning, they would not have gone on to develop an anxiety disorder. It is an ongoing tragedy that early intervention strategies are rarely considered, or used to minimise or prevent the development of an anxiety disorder. Many of the treatment options available are reactive rather than proactive, and inadvertently contribute to the development and perpetuation of anxiety disorders.

While many people are committed to caring for their physical health, most of us are not really concerned about our mental health. Working with early intervention strategies means making this commitment to ourselves. Our mental health is just as important as our physical health and early intervention strategies can assist us in protecting it. Although there are no specific resources available for early intervention, there is still much you can do to prevent or minimise the possible development of a disorder.

Understanding

The first question everyone asks is 'What is happening to me?' As I said before, the words 'panic attacks' and 'anxiety' do not describe the actual feeling state of these experiences. The feeling state is much more than these three words can convey. This is why it is so important for us to learn and understand the dynamics of our experience. The more we understand, the less fear we have, which makes our panic attacks and anxiety easier to control. Knowledge and understanding of our experience give us power.

In many instances our doctor doesn't give us an adequate explanation of our experience. We may be told we are having panic attacks or experiencing anxiety and just be given a prescription for medication. This leaves many people feeling confused and frightened. Often they feel too awkward or embarrassed to ask their doctor for a more detailed explanation. This is a big mistake! There is no reason to feel awkward or embarrassed. Doctors see many people with panic attacks and anxiety so it is important we do not let these feelings prevent us from asking for more detailed information. We may not realise that some doctors assume we know and understand what is happening to us, and may be surprised that we don't.

While we may be given a prescription for medication, it is also important that we ask our doctor about early intervention strategies such as cognitive therapy. Cognitive behavioural therapy (CBT) can assist us in learning to work with, and control, our thoughts that create so much of our distress and confusion. If our doctor doesn't offer, or isn't able to provide, such strategies, we can ask to be referred to a cognitive behavioural therapist. A CB therapist will assist with these strategies.

Knowledge and understanding about our panic attacks and anxiety will help us to accept and work with our experience more easily. Anxiety disorder organisations, either local or via the Internet, can provide additional information and referral to cognitive behavioural therapists, and may also be able to provide telephone support, access to support groups and other resources.

The second question everyone asks is: 'Why is this happening to me?' Research suggests there is a 'genetic contribution to the development of panic disorder' (APA 1994). It is not unusual for us to discover that other family members may have had or still have the disorder. In our parents' and grandparents' generation, people were never diagnosed and they coped with it as best they could. In previous generations the disorder may sometimes have been 'hiding' behind an alcohol dependency or behind what we consider to be 'eccentric' behaviour in a family member.

The genetic aspect always raises secondary questions: 'What about my children? Will they start to have panic attacks?' If they do, early intervention strategies will be able to minimise, or prevent, the development of panic disorder. Hopefully, resources for this will be more readily available in the future.

Panic attacks and/or anxiety can be triggered by any number of reasons—a major life stress, a build-up of stress, physical illness, menopause, influenza or another virus, the birth of a child, studying for exams, marijuana or other similar drugs.

On occasion there may be a time lag of up to twelve months between a major life stress and the initial panic attack. The effects of the major life stress can be compounded by ongoing day-to-day stress, which ultimately triggers our first panic attack or our anxiety. Yet, it is not so much the stress itself that creates our distress as the way we perceive and deal with the stress that triggers our panic attacks/anxiety. I discuss this further at the end of this chapter.

Sometimes there doesn't appear to be any reason at all for the development of anxiety or panic attacks. This only adds to our confusion. We usually don't recognise the various stresses in our lives, or simply write them off as not being a factor. It can help to make a list of past and current events in our lives. When we actually see it written down, the reason for the panic attacks and anxiety becomes obvious.

Initial fears

One of the major reasons why people go on to develop an anxiety disorder is that they are frightened their doctor has made a mistake in the diagnosis. They may also fear their clinical test results have been mixed up with someone else's. This fear is a direct consequence of the 'feeling' experience of a panic attack or anxiety and the actual words used to describe it: 'panic attack', 'anxiety'. These words seem inadequate to explain the force of the experience and so we feel there must be something else wrong with us which has been overlooked.

It is important to discuss this fear with the doctor. Again we may be too embarrassed or perhaps frightened of doing so, but we need to. The fear that there may have been a mistake only fuels our fear, which makes us more vulnerable to further panic attacks and anxiety.

Some people will get a second opinion and this can be extremely helpful if it assists us in accepting the diagnosis. It is when we seek a third or fourth or perhaps tenth opinion that we need to stop and begin the process of believing it and accepting the diagnosis. If we don't believe and accept it, then our fear can be the major driver of the development of an anxiety disorder.

We all need to understand and accept the sensations and symptoms of our panic attacks and our anxiety for what they are— panic and anxiety. Nothing more. They can make us feel as if we are going to die, have a heart attack, go insane, lose control or embarrass ourselves in some way. 'Can make us feel as if' are the operative words. We do not die, go insane or lose control through panic and anxiety. This is what a panic attack feels like. This is what high anxiety feels like. We need to believe it and accept it.

Many of us get caught up in the thoughts . . . 'This is not me, I am not like this. I am the strong one in the family. I am extroverted/the life of the party. How can this be happening to me?' Most of us think this! Being strong, which we are, or being extroverted, which some of us can be, does not exempt us from panic and anxiety. Anxiety disorders are equal opportunity disorders. They do not discriminate!

Our confusion and fears can be compounded if we tell other people. We get caught up in their exclamations: 'Don't be silly, you're not like that! You are too strong.' This adds to our confusion and fear because we think that society's perception, and perhaps ours, is that people with anxiety are 'weak' and should 'pull themselves together'.

I say 'society's perception' because it is not as rigid or as judgmental as we may believe. Official figures show that 9.7% of the population has an anxiety disorder (ABS 1997). My rule of thumb, which has yet to be disproved, is that we will know three other people, who are not family members, who have an anxiety disorder. These three people are hiding it from us because they are worried about what we will think of them.

The fear and stigma that mental illness itself carries within the community is also a factor. We begin to feel extremely ashamed, especially if our panic attacks or anxiety increase no matter how hard we try to 'pull ourselves together'. What we don't realise is that the shame we feel about ourselves only increases our fear; this in turn increases our anxiety, which continues to fuel our fear, and round and round we go. Panic attacks, anxiety, anxiety disorders or mental illness are nothing to be ashamed of. We have all heard this said before and, while we may agree with it in relation to other people, the time has now come for us to begin to believe the truth of it in relation to ourselves.

The fact is that we don't have anything to be ashamed about. Millions of people worldwide experience panic attacks and anxiety. The more we resist accepting our experience, the more we fuel the potential for developing an anxiety disorder. Knowledge, understanding and acceptance of our experience diminishes this potential.

Medication

The first form of treatment most people are offered for their panic attacks is medication. In fact, some people are offered medication on their first visit to the doctor. While medication can assist in easing our symptoms, it is not a cure. Many people find that medication 'masks' their symptoms and, once it is withdrawn, the panic attacks and anxiety reappear. Medication is not necessarily an early intervention strategy. If we have just begun to experience panic attacks or anxiety we are in an ideal position to learn to manage them ourselves, without becoming caught up in a possible medication cycle.

While most people do not want to take medication there can be a time and place for it. It is not a sign we are weak or a failure. Some people find that medication helps to ease their symptoms while they concentrate on learning new cognitive skills. Once they have withdrawn their medication under supervision of their doctor, they can then use their cognitive skills to manage any further panic and anxiety.

If we do decide to take medication it is our responsibility to ensure we make an informed decision about it. We need to know the expected outcomes, the side effects and the length of time we will be using the medication. We also need to know the possibility of addiction and of any withdrawal or 'discontinuation' reactions (BMJ 1998).

It is also important to know of possible interactions with other prescribed medications or over-the-counter medications such as cold and flu preparations, and of any interactions with herbal products or alcohol. Women who are pregnant or planning a pregnancy, and those who are breast-feeding, also need to know if there is any possible risk to the baby. Once we have this knowledge we can make an informed decision in conjunction with our doctor as to the most suitable treatment options for us.

Cognitive behavioural therapy (CBT)

If we choose cognitive behavioural therapy as either our only treatment option, or in conjunction with medication, then we need to do the necessary work involved in learning to manage and control our thought processes. I discuss CBT in detail in Chapter 4. It is pointless committing to a CBT option if we are not prepared to do the work. Some people will begin to use CBT and then give it up as soon as their panic attacks or anxiety diminish. They then become further traumatised if the panic and anxiety reappear—which it can do if their cognitive skills are still rudimentary.

While some people may not want to use medication for the management of their panic and anxiety, they will use it to relax. This is giving away our power! If we are committed to learning to manage our panic and anxiety ourselves then we need to learn and become disciplined in a relaxation technique. Meditation or relaxation assists us in reducing stress levels. This is in part taking care of our mental health.

Stress

I made the comment earlier that it is not so much a particular stressful event that creates our distress but rather the way we perceive and deal with the stressful situation. A classic example of this is the fear and distress we feel in relation to our panic and anxiety. When we have our first panic attack and don't know what is happening to us, fear of it is a natural response. Once we are diagnosed and know what is happening, we need to begin to accept our experience for what it is. Yet we don't do that. We see the experience as threatening in some way. We become engulfed in a tidal wave of fear which only creates further distress, and we become caught in the anxiety and panic cycle very quickly. We deal with it by worrying about it, and then by worrying about the symptoms of our worry!

We do this in most stressful situations. We perceive them and deal with them in ways that only create further stress. The origin of this action is our perception of our self and who we think we should be. We deal with stressful situations from the perspective of how we think we *should* deal with them, rather than how we *could* deal with them. Unknowingly, this can be detrimental to our mental health.

Self-esteem

Our perception of our self and who we think we should be impacts on our self-esteem. Many of us have low self-esteem, and it is this low self-esteem and lack of a sense of self that ultimately underpin our panic attacks and anxiety. Healthy self-esteem and an anxiety disorder are mutually exclusive.

As part of a commitment to our mental health we can address the problems inherent in being who 'we think we should be'. Working on these issues will help us to sustain a healthier self-esteem which supports long-term prevention of an anxiety disorder.

In summary, there is much we can do to help ourselves prevent or minimise the potential development of an anxiety disorder. These include:

- a commitment to ourselves and our mental health
- a detailed understanding of our panic attacks and anxiety
- knowing why they happen
- knowing how they happen
- accepting them for what they are, not what we think they are!
- accepting ourselves for having panic and anxiety
- making informed decisions about treatment options
- committing to our chosen treatment option/s
- assessing our self-esteem and its impact on how we deal with stress
- developing a healthier sense of self

These topics are discussed in detail in the following chapters but, from this point, the focus of the book changes. Most people have never been able to access early intervention strategies and they have gone on to develop an anxiety disorder. In the following chapters I discuss anxiety disorders and techniques for recovery that can also be used as early intervention strategies.

CHAPTER 2

ANXIETY DISORDERS

Anxiety disorders were first recognised as a discrete group of disorders in 1980 by the American Psychiatric Association (APA 1980). Anxiety disorders include panic disorder, social phobia, post-traumatic stress disorder, obsessive compulsive disorder and generalised anxiety disorder.

Many people are surprised when they realise that anxiety disorders represent the largest mental health problem in the general population. While there is now much more publicity about panic attacks and anxiety, anxiety disorders are still hidden within the community. When we begin to develop an anxiety disorder, we feel as if we are the only one in the world experiencing this level of distress. We are not being narcissistic. It is more that we can't believe other people could be feeling this degree of distress and it not be more widely acknowledged in the community.

Anxiety disorders affect people right across the socioeconomic spectrum and across all age groups. While many people will develop an anxiety disorder between their late teens and mid thirties, children can also develop a disorder and so can people in their forties right through to their eighties.

People often ask me if the increase in the number of people with an anxiety disorder is due to the escalating pressures and demands of life. While this is a factor, the main reason for the increase is that, in the recent past, many people were simply not being diagnosed at all and lived their life suffering from 'nerves'.

Causes

There are various theories as to the cause of anxiety disorders. Physiological research suspects that a chemical imbalance may be involved although researchers are unsure whether a chemical imbalance is the cause or a result of the panic attack (APA 1990). Behaviour theories suggest that anxiety disorders are learned behaviours and recovery means unlearning the previous limiting behaviour (APA 1990). Psychoanalytic theory postulates that anxiety stems from subconscious unresolved conflicts that began during childhood (APA 1990).

This conflicting information about the cause of anxiety disorders makes it difficult for us to come to an informed decision about the most suitable treatment. It is possible that the three schools of thought are each partly correct, and that viewed together they form a whole picture of cause and effect (APA 1990).

Panic attacks

The experience of panic attacks is central to four of the anxiety disorders, with generalised anxiety disorder the exception. While the disorders were recognised in 1980, it wasn't until 1994 that a more definitive understanding of panic attacks and anxiety disorders emerged (APA 1994). Prior to this no distinction was made between types of panic attacks and the relevant anxiety disorder. Panic attacks were seen more as a phobic response to particular situations and places, yet for people with panic disorder this was not the case. People were not frightened of situations or places. They were frightened of having a panic attack. It didn't matter where they were or what they were doing, it was the fear of actually having an attack that was the problem.

In 1994 three separate and distinct types of panic attacks were identified and their relationship to particular anxiety disorders was defined (APA 1994).

UNCUED (SPONTANEOUS) PANIC ATTACKS

The experience of an uncued attack is the central feature of panic disorder. This type of panic attack is not triggered by situations and places. It occurs spontaneously, 'out of the blue', irrespective of what the person may be doing at the time. These attacks can also happen when people are relaxed, reading a book, watching television, when they are going to sleep at night; or they can be woken from sleep with an attack. Attacks can feel completely overwhelming, physically and psychologically, and many people do feel as if they are having a heart attack, or dying or going insane.

What isn't discussed in any detail in the literature on anxiety disorders is the fact that the spontaneous panic attack can have a number of distinguishing symptoms that differ from the other two types of panic attacks. My colleagues and I have found in our own research (Arthur-Jones & Fox 1994) that these symptoms are, in many cases, the reason why people panic. That is, the symptoms come first and people panic in response to them, as opposed to the symptoms being part of the actual panic. I discuss this in detail below.

CUED (SPECIFIC) PANIC ATTACKS

Unlike the experience of a spontaneous attack, the cued attack does relate to, and is triggered by, specific situations or places. The cued attack can be one of the components of social anxiety, post-traumatic stress disorder or obsessive compulsive disorder.

SITUATIONALLY PREDISPOSED PANIC ATTACKS

Some people may be predisposed to having panic attacks in some situations and/or places. The attack is not necessarily always triggered by the particular situation or place—it may happen on some occasions and not on others. People with spontaneous panic attacks may go on to develop this type of attack.

Panic disorder

Panic disorder is the fear of having a spontaneous panic attack, *fear* being the operative word. It is the *fear* of having a spontaneous panic attack that is the driving force in the development of panic disorder.

Some people may only ever have one panic attack while others may have intermittent attacks throughout their life, in both cases this does not necessarily mean they will go on to develop panic disorder.

Panic disorder is diagnosed after a person has experienced 'at least two' spontaneous panic attacks followed by one month of 'persistent concern' about having another one (APA 1994). It is the 'persistent concern', our fear, that not only causes much of our distress but also makes us more vulnerable to having another attack. And many of us do. It is not unusual for people to begin to have two or more panic attacks a day and to experience pervasive anxiety in anticipation of having another one.

Recovery for so many of us has been the loss of the fear of having one of these attacks. Once we can lose our fear we 'lose' the disorder, and lose our ongoing anxiety about having another attack.

Social phobia

People with social phobia are frightened of making a fool of themselves or embarrassing themselves in some way because they fear being judged in a negative way by other people (APA 1994).

They may fear social occasions or simply talking with other people in day-to-day situations. They may fear eating in front of other people, signing their name or writing in front of others. People can suffer extreme anxiety in these situations, or simply in anticipating them. They may have a panic attack as a result. This panic attack is specific to their fear that they may embarrass, or make a fool of, themselves in some way.

Post-traumatic stress disorder

Post-traumatic stress disorder can develop following an event or events in which the person 'experienced, witnessed or was confronted' (APA 1994) with a situation that was life-threatening to themselves and/or other people. This can include victims of violent crime, rape, a serious accident, active war duty or being civilians in a war zone, natural disasters such as bushfires, cyclones or earthquakes.

People may have ongoing persistent thoughts about the experience. They may have flashbacks in which they believe they are actually living through the event again, or nightmares in which they relive the experience. Many people will have a cued panic attack in situations or places similar to, or reminiscent of, the actual event.

Panic disorder can be secondary to post-traumatic stress disorder. On occasions people will seek treatment for their panic disorder but will be too frightened or ashamed to speak of the traumatic event or events that precipitated it. This is especially so in matters relating to childhood abuse. One English study showed that 63.6% of young women with panic disorder who were interviewed for the study came from 'difficult childhood backgrounds', which included 'parental indifference, sexual and physical abuse' (Brown & Harris 1993).

Obsessive compulsive disorder

Obsessive compulsive disorder means being obsessed by 'persistent ideas, thoughts, impulses, or images that cause marked anxiety or distress' (APA 1994). Unlike generalised anxiety disorder, which is based on 'real life' concerns, the obsessive thoughts can be a fear of contamination by germs or a fear the person might harm other people, or act in a socially unacceptable way.

Other people may need to have everything arranged in a particular way, or redo certain jobs a number of times. Some people may feel the need to repeat a name or number or phrase constantly. Others may continually check to see if they have locked their house or car, or if they have turned off domestic appliances. Some people may hoard unwanted or useless items. These compulsions can be so severe that the person becomes totally restricted by them and is unable to lead a normal life.

Generalised anxiety disorder

Generalised anxiety disorder is diagnosed when a person experiences 'anxiety and worry' (APA 1994) for at least six months over particular real life events such as marital or financial problems. Most people with this disorder have been worriers all their life and feel powerless to stop the endless cycle of worry.

Combinations

It is not unusual for people to have fears and symptoms from all the disorders. People with panic disorder usually have ongoing anxiety. They may also have aspects of obsessive compulsive disorder, social anxiety and, in some instances, post-traumatic stress disorder.

CASE HISTORIES

Carolyn

It had been a long and difficult week. Carolyn was glad she now had some time to herself. She curled up on the lounge with a book she had been wanting to read. As she relaxed she felt the tension ease from her body and she felt herself drifting into sleep. Without warning, she felt a wave of incredible energy surge through her body. As it moved through her, her heart rate doubled, she had difficulty breathing, she felt lightheaded and dizzy, a wave of nausea swept over her and she began to perspire. She jumped up and ran outside to her husband. 'Help me,' she cried. 'Something is happening to me, I don't know what, but something is very wrong.'

Alex

Alex disliked staff meetings and social get-togethers and did what he could to avoid them. He felt more comfortable just doing his job and avoiding personal interaction with other staff. Now the new owners of the business had arranged a dinner for all staff and their partners and, like it or not, Alex had to go. He had been feeling uncomfortable all day and he knew his anxiety levels were very high. As he and his wife sat down at their table the people next to them began to make conversation. Alex's heart began to race, his breathing became short and shallow, he began to perspire heavily and his hands trembled violently. As he tried to control it, he thought to himself, 'I shouldn't have come. This always happens every time I am in this situation.'

Jessica

Jessica turned on the ignition of her car. She was feeling very anxious. Is it going to happen today? As she pulled out of her driveway she tried to rationalise with herself for the hundredth time. She wasn't frightened of driving—in fact, she used to enjoy driving before she began to have spontaneous panic attacks. But there was one set of traffic lights where she would sometimes have an attack. There was no pattern to it. Sometimes it happened, sometimes it didn't. Sometimes she would have an attack after she had driven through the traffic lights; on other days there were no attacks at all. Someone had told her she was frightened of that particular intersection, but she thought that was ridiculous. She was frightened of the attacks and their unpredictable nature, it had nothing to do with the intersection.

Symptoms

If you haven't been diagnosed as having panic attacks or a panic-related anxiety disorder but think this may be what you are experiencing, speak to a doctor. Don't self-diagnose. You need to know exactly what it is you are trying to recover from.

Many of our symptoms are a direct result of the 'fight-and-flight' response. This is an automatic response within the body that is activated in times of danger. It assists us either to stay and fight the danger or to run away from it. The problem is, we are not in actual danger. The 'danger' is being created by the way we think and our body responds accordingly.

The symptoms of anxiety can be quite varied, with any number of symptoms being experienced at the same time. A panic attack is diagnosed when we experience four or more of these symptoms (APA 1994). The most common ones are a rapid or pounding

heartbeat, palpitations, 'missed' heartbeats, chest pain, hyper-ventilation, difficulty in breathing, an inability to take a deep breath, a feeling breathing will stop altogether, a choking sensation, tightening of the throat, indigestion, churning or burning in the stomach, dizziness, giddiness, feeling faint, lightheaded, nausea, pins and needles, diarrhoea, shaking, trembling, dry mouth, excessive perspiration, neck ache, headache, flushed face.

People with panic disorder can also report left arm pain and jaw pain. Most experience a number of dissociative symptoms such as depersonalisation (the feeling of being detached from the body), derealisation (where nothing appears to be real, or feeling as though looking through a white or grey mist), other visual disturbances including stationary objects appearing to move, tunnel vision, intolerance to sound and intolerance to light (Arthur-Jones & Fox 1994).

Sometimes these symptoms are our constant companions. Not just for a few minutes or hours at a time, sometimes they can be chronic for months or years. To confuse the issue further, people may experience different symptoms and sensations in their anxiety and with each panic attack (Arthur-Jones & Fox 1994).

Many people experience a number of effects as a result of their anxiety disorder. These can include fatigue or overwhelming exhaustion, loss of concentration, loss of appetite, loss of libido and, in some instances, loss of feelings towards family and friends.

Dissociation

Another theory my colleagues and I have been investigating is the role played by dissociation in spontaneous panic attacks. From my research and experience, the ability to dissociate is extremely common in people who experience spontaneous panic attacks. In fact, as they begin to understand their ability to dissociate, they become aware that it is their dissociation that triggers the feelings of panic (Arthur-Jones & Fox 1994)

Dissociation can also be described as altered or discrete states of consciousness or trance states. Dissociation can be an 'accepted expression of cultural or religious experience in many societies' (APA 1994). A leading expert in altered or discrete states, Dr Charles Tart (1972), comments that many other cultures 'believe that almost every normal adult has the ability to go into a trance state'.

Individuals in some societies induce trance states not only by meditation but by fasting, sleep deprivation and other forms of physiological stress. For those of us who have the ability to dissociate, major stress can make us more vulnerable to these states. Or stress can be a cause of our not eating properly or of losing sleep, which in turn increases our vulnerability to them.

The ability to dissociate is not harmful in itself, but our lack of understanding of the phenomenon can lead to acute anxiety and panic. Although some people with panic disorder report they are not frightened of these sensations, others are and the fear contributes to the feeling of going insane or loss of control.

DISSOCIATION AND SPONTANEOUS PANIC ATTACKS

It has been assumed that dissociation is an effect of a panic attack and that some people use these states as a form of 'escape' from the anxiety or the attack itself. While I have seen this in a few cases, most people are aware it is the dissociation itself that triggers the panic (Arthur-Jones & Fox 1994).

Some people experience depersonalisation or derealisation or other dissociative sensations first and panic as a result of these sensations. Others report these sensations together with a feeling like an electric shock, or an intense burning and tingling sensation, moving through the body. Some report a feeling like a wave of unusual energy surging through them (Arthur-Jones & Fox 1994). This wave is usually experienced as beginning in the feet, surging through the body, over the head and back down through the body again (Arthur-Jones & Fox 1994). Or it is likened to a white-hot flame, starting 'just below the breast bone, passing through the chest, up the spine, into the face, down the arms and even down to the groin and to the tips of the toes' (Weekes 1992).

One psychiatrist quotes a description of a panic attack by one of his patients. The attack begins with 'a tingling feeling going up my spine which enters my head and causes a sensation of faintness and nausea. I feel I'm going to lose control or lose consciousness. I thought I was going to die and started to panic . . .' (Hafner 1986). Notice how his patient separates the attack from the feelings of panic. This is important.

Another psychiatrist describes the attack as being associated to a 'rushing sensation of a hot flash surging through the body'. People may experience a sensation that is 'sometimes associated with a sick feeling and a sensation of fading out from the world'. This faintness is more like a 'whiteout' than a 'blackout' and the head may literally 'feel light'. The fear of this attack is then followed by the fight-and-flight response (Sheehan 1983). Again, notice the separation between the precipitating sensations and the fight-and-flight response.

From my own experience and those of my clients, the rushing sensation, the hot flash, the tingling or the electric shock sensation happen as part of the overall dissociative experience, and we panic in reaction to this.

For those of us who do dissociate, learning to see this separation from the feelings of panic is an important step in recovery and I will return to this point shortly.

People who do dissociate 'may display high hypnotisability and high dissociative capacity' (APA 1994). The dissociative sensations are the effects of an alteration of consciousness which can be similar to the alteration of consciousness when deeply relaxed or meditating or in hypnotic states.

Many people report they can be fully relaxed when they have an attack and one research study confirmed this. The study looked at EEG activity in people with panic disorder and found, to the researchers' surprise, a 'paradoxical positive correlation between increases in slow wave EEG and increasing anxiety' while the patient was at rest (Knott 1990).

'Slow wave activity' indicates a very relaxed state. The question is how can we be relaxed and anxious at the same time? The study concluded that 'replication of increases in slow wave activity in further studies would suggest psychobiological disturbances in panic disorder are not merely normal emotions expressed in inappropriate contexts' (Knott 1990). This study indicates that our overall experience of an attack is more than the spontaneous arousal of the fight-and-flight response, normally viewed as the reason for a spontaneous panic attack.

Nocturnal panic attacks

The theme of Knott's study is also demonstrated in the literature on nocturnal panic attacks. Many of us are woken at night by these attacks. Research suggests the 'sleep' panic attack occurs 'during the transition from stage two to stage three sleep' (Uhde 1994). The research also stipulates that the attack is not a result of dreams or nightmares (Uhde 1994), but happens on the alteration of consciousness.

'Sensory shocks' that can accompany the hypnogogic (first) stage of sleep or the transition from dreaming sleep were first noted in 1890. Researchers describe them as 'an upward surge of indescribable nature, an electric sort of feeling ascending from the abdomen to the head sometimes followed by bodily jerks or a violent explosion and/or a flash of light'. The researchers also note that a sense of alarm, together with a cold sweat, laboured breathing and tachycardia, often follows (Oswald 1962).

And for many of us this sense of 'alarm' can be the 1990s definition of our panic! Our attacks are usually interpreted within the biological model, as the fight-or-flight response. Within the psychological model it is thought that people have more time to think about their anxiety symptoms when they are relaxed, thereby actuating the fight-and-flight response. The possibility we may be dissociating first is never considered. As one researcher points out, the transition into the trance states can occur in a split second (Putman 1989) and it is in that split second that we can go from feeling relaxed to total panic.

Inducing dissociative states

Inducing dissociative states when we are vulnerable to them is incredibly easy. The most common way is by staring—at the computer, at the television screen, at a book. We stare while driving—at the traffic lights, the car in front of us, at the road ahead. We stare at people when we are talking to them, we stare ahead when we are out walking, we stare while we are waiting for an elevator. When we are vulnerable we can induce a trance state very quickly and without realising it. Without warning we can feel the sensations of dissociation.

In Eastern traditions, open-eyed meditation is an advanced meditation technique, usually taught only to skilled practitioners (Brunton 1965). Yet many of us unconsciously practise a similar method of 'meditation'. In many cases we induce a dissociative state and panic as the result of the sensations. Our self-absorption can be absolute, and this self-absorption is similar to other meditation techniques. We need to be aware that our self-absorption can be significant enough to also induce dissociative states.

Some people report that fluorescent lighting can also induce a dissociative state (Arthur-Jones & Fox 1994). This is one of the reasons why people can have so much difficulty in shopping centres. The sheer brightness, the glare of the lights can be overwhelming and can induce a dissociative state. Some people can actually see the moment-to-moment flickering of the lights which can also induce trance states.

Fight-and-flight response

Many of us who experience dissociative sensations know they are not part of the fight-and-flight response. We have all been in situations where the fight-and-flight response has been activated—perhaps a near miss with another car while driving, or waiting for surgery, any situation that can produce fear. People with a background of abuse know all too well the feelings of fear and the accompanying symptoms of the fight-and-flight response. Even if the fight-and-flight response were activated spontaneously, we would be able to recognise it. We would not react with total fear if our experience was simply that of the fight-and-flight response.

The description of panic disorder is 'the presence of recurrent unexpected panic attacks followed by at least one month of persistent concern about having another panic attack' (APA 1994). Our persistent concern triggers the fight-and-flight response and adds ferocity to our overall experience. Once the attack subsides, the fight-and-flight response is continually activated by our fear of having another attack. It is the fight-and-flight response that creates our anxiety symptoms.

For me and other people, recovery means that we may occasionally experience an attack. In other words, we may dissociate when we are tired or stressed but, instead of reacting with fear and panic, we can now break the dissociated state and allow any physical effects—the 'indescribable surge'—to happen. When we do this, the attack disappears as quickly as it comes. Recovery is a matter of learning to change our perception of these particular attacks, learning to see them and control them without fear. When we can do this, we are able to think 'So what?' instead of 'What if?' I discuss this further in Chapter 9.

CHAPTER 3

SECONDARY CONDITIONS

As we saw in the first chapter, part of the overall problem in understanding the severity of anxiety disorders lies in the words 'anxiety' and 'panic attack'. There is a marked difference between the 'normal' experience of anxiety and the anxiety that becomes so extreme that people are disabled by it.

Anxiety

Everyone has been anxious at some time. Some people have difficulty accepting that the experience of an anxiety disorder is different from their own individual experience of anxiety. Their anxiety may not have affected them to any great extent; it passed of its own accord and was no longer a problem. As a result, they find it difficult to accept that a person with an anxiety disorder experiences something different from normal anxiety. It is from this perspective that some people label others with an anxiety disorder as 'weak' and tell them to 'pull themselves together'.

The same applies to the words 'panic attack'. Often, when I am talking publicly about panic attacks, someone will make the comment: 'I know what that is like. I had a panic attack the other day. I was running late for work and could not find my car keys.' While they may have panicked, the experience of a panic attack is not that simple or straightforward.

People with panic disorder—and sometimes people with one of the other anxiety disorders—do not recognise their symptoms as indicative of anxiety and panic attacks, especially if they have a dissociative component to their attacks.

The attacks

Everyone who experiences spontaneous panic attack remembers their first attack, where they were, what they were doing and how it felt. There is no other experience to compare it with. For most of us, the attack appears to have little or nothing to do with any personal or environmental situation. Even if we are very distressed about a particular situation, it can seem to us there is no direct relationship between the situation and the attack. In contrast, with social phobia, obsessive compulsive disorder and post-traumatic stress disorder, people may recognise the driving force behind their attack as it is usually specific to a particular situation.

Most people who experience a spontaneous attack go straight to a doctor or the nearest hospital, sometimes by ambulance, because the attack actually feels like a heart attack. We go through the standard clinical tests which show there is nothing physically wrong. This can happen not just once or twice, but maybe quite a number of times!

The diagnosis that there is nothing physically wrong with us does not bring relief. The panic attack can be so severe and the physical reaction so extreme, it is difficult to believe there is not a physical cause. It is impossible not to feel frightened, especially if there appears to be little or no relationship between the panic attack and our current personal situation.

It is from this situation that the first of many 'what ifs' is born. 'What if the doctor has made a mistake?' 'What if there is really something wrong which has been overlooked?' 'What if the test results have been mixed up?' Our fear pushes our anxiety level higher and we may in fact have another panic attack. The cycle of panic and anxiety has begun. We can't imagine why, if we are only suffering from stress or anxiety, we can't 'pull ourselves together'. In fact, the harder we try, the worse we become.

The primary fears

The primary fears are usually established with the first panic attack. The first and most common fear is 'I'm having a heart attack' and/or 'I am going to die'. The second is 'I am going insane', and the third is 'I'm going to lose control of myself' which could mean 'I'm going to faint', 'I'm going to make a fool of myself", 'I will vomit', 'I will have an attack of diarrhoea', or, literally, 'I am going to lose control'.

From the primary fears come flow-on fears. We begin to avoid situations and places for fear of experiencing a panic attack or panic-like symptoms. We may find we are too frightened to drive the car, go to the supermarket, go out to dinner, entertain friends. We may struggle trying to meet our daily work and family commitments, not because we are frightened of any of them, but because we are frightened we may have a panic attack.

As I said in the last chapter, prior to the introduction of the three different types of panic attacks, a panic attack was seen more as a phobic response to situations and places. Our avoidance behaviour was interpreted as being a fear of a particular situation or place and our panic attacks as a phobic response to it. In the past, behavioural treatments tried to persuade us to lose our fear of the situation or place. The fear of having a spontaneous panic attack was not considered and so many people struggled in trying to recover.

CASE HISTORIES

Paul

Paul sat on the side of the hospital bed. He was being discharged after a night in hospital for observation because he felt as if he were having a heart attack. The specialist had told him he had not had a heart attack, but a panic attack. Paul had tried to tell the specialist that of course he had panicked. He had felt terrible and thought he was going to die. Surely, he thought, it was normal to panic under those circumstances.

Julie

The end of Julie's shift was in sight. Another hour and she could go home, but first she had to hand over to the nurses on afternoon shift. She felt her stomach tighten and her anxiety increased. Julie had never had problems talking in front of other people before but the thought of hand-over today terrified her. She remembered the last few weeks and how it had become increasingly difficult for her to appear 'normal'. Julie had had her first panic attack at work. Although she knew what was wrong with her she was having enormous difficulty trying to 'pull herself together'. She couldn't control what was happening to her. She knew the other nurses wouldn't understand if they found out. Julie felt she couldn't go to any of the doctors at the hospital where she worked, as she was frightened they would make her resign.

Sam

Sam drove his truck out of the depot and onto the road that would take him to the freeway. He wiped the perspiration from his forehead. His hands were trembling. He had to keep going. This time he couldn't go back to the depot and say he was sick. Once more and he knew he would lose his job. His stomach was churning. The further away he was from the depot the worse he became. All Sam wanted to do was go home. He didn't know how much more he could take. Over the last twelve months he had stopped doing most of the things he used to enjoy—playing or watching sport, having a few drinks with friends or going for a drive with his family. Now he just stayed at home. It took all his energy just to get to work and get through each day.

Michael

Michael had been on stress leave for eight weeks and was due to return to work. He had spoken to his rehabilitation counsellor because his condition, far from easing, was becoming worse. Since being on leave his panic attacks had increased and his anxiety level was very high. Every time he left the familiar surroundings of his neighbourhood he would be overcome with the fear of having another panic attack. More often than not he would have one. The consulting doctor had said Michael was just suffering from stress and that he should think seriously about 'getting his act together' and getting back to work. After all, said the doctor, Michael was lucky to have a job to go back to. No one seemed to understand that all Michael wanted to do was return to work. He certainly didn't like what was happening to him. He had always been conscientious at work and had rarely taken time off. He wondered if he should resign. He thought it would be better than having to face his counsellor's and the doctor's doubt.

Lack of understanding

In the past, and even now, an overall lack of understanding and effective treatment options plays a significant role in the development of anxiety disorders and the secondary conditions associated with them. These include agoraphobia, major depression, prescribed-drug addiction and alcohol dependency. As suggested in the opening chapter, these secondary conditions can be prevented with early intervention strategies.

Many of the treatment methods we have used are either only partially effective or not effective at all. In many cases, the responsibility for ineffective treatment is placed back on to us. We are not trying to 'pull ourselves together', we are 'obviously getting something out of being this way', we are 'weak and have no will power' or 'no strength of character'. In many cases we take this on board and mentally abuse ourselves by thinking that we are weak, we are a failure, we are hopeless. Ineffective treatment does not mean we are ineffective people.

How many times have we heard the expression 'Pull yourself together'? If it were that easy, we would have done so long before. The irony is, the harder we try to 'pull ourselves together', the harder we fight what is happening to us, the worse we become.

Depression

With little or no effective treatment, our lifestyle as we knew it can be totally disrupted or destroyed by our anxiety disorder. Many people go on to develop a major depression in reaction to their disorder. Until recently, this depression could be diagnosed as the primary disorder, leaving the anxiety disorder itself untreated. This has resulted in people struggling with an anxiety disorder for many years. Even now some people are being diagnosed as having a primary depressive disorder while their anxiety disorder remains untreated.

Suicide

The symptoms of depression can be very similar to panic and anxiety symptoms and compound our overall level of distress. The disintegration of ourselves and our lives through the effects of the disorder and its secondary conditions brings a sense of hopelessness and helplessness. Suddenly, in major contradiction to the fear of dying, we may find ourselves contemplating or attempting suicide. It begins to appear the only way out. It is not.

Many of us will not discuss these thoughts and feelings with family members or our doctor. The sense of 'this is not me', and the shame and humiliation that we feel, counteract our most desperate plea for help. Most of us would never have thought of ourselves as ever being suicidal. The realisation we are even considering suicide creates further fear and confusion, which in turn isolates us even further. If we do find ourselves thinking of suicide it is very important to speak to our doctor and family immediately. Suicide is not the answer. Recovery is—and we can recover with effective treatment.

Agoraphobia: avoidance behaviour

Without adequate understanding and treatment we do not effectively control what is happening to us, so we begin to develop other forms of control in an effort to ease our situation. Ironically and tragically, many of the controls we use actually become secondary conditions and help to compound and perpetuate our disorder. This in turn perpetuates the myth that we are not doing anything to help ourselves.

Agoraphobia is one such control. Developing agoraphobia has meant a lifetime of limitation for many people. Until panic disorder was recognised in 1980, agoraphobia was considered to be the primary problem. Agoraphobia used to be defined as a fear of open spaces and/or the marketplace and the olderstyle behavioural treatment programs focused on this. But we were not frightened by open spaces or the 'marketplace'—we were frightened of having a panic attack in any space or place! It didn't matter where we were or what we were doing, the fear was always with us.

Now agoraphobia in panic disorder is recognised as 'anxiety about being in situations or places from which escape might be difficult or embarrassing or in which help may not be available in the event of having an uncued or situationally predisposed attack' (APA 1994). And/or 'The situation is endured with marked distress or anxiety . . . or may require the presence of a companion' (APA 1994).

Agoraphobia associated with social phobia is avoidance behaviour 'limited to' social situations. In obsessive compulsive disorder it is avoidance behaviour relating to the particular obsessive thoughts. In post-traumatic stress disorder, agoraphobia is seen as avoidance of 'stimuli' related to the trauma. Although the avoidance behaviour is limited to the particular disorder, it can be all encompassing and people may become housebound.

Some people become housebound, totally avoiding certain situations and/or places after the first spontaneous attack. In other cases, the avoidance behaviour may be gradual, becoming increasingly restricting, or it may be permanently limited to one or two situations and/or places. People may have occasional panic attacks for years before avoidance behaviour sets in. In this case, the onset of avoidance behaviour is not a result of the panic attack itself, but is usually a fear of a new symptom of anxiety.

Agoraphobia can affect people in different degrees. It can also affect the same person in different degrees at different times. It is a multi-faceted and multi-contradictory condition.

Our avoidance behaviour may appear to others that we are not trying to overcome the disorder, but giving in to it. We are not. Our avoidance behaviour is a defence against the disorder, and without early intervention strategies it has been one of the few controls we've had.

AN OVERALL DEFENCE

The development of avoidance behaviour means that everyday normal situations and/or places can become associated with anxiety and panic attacks. Although we are not frightened of the particular situation or place, we avoid them as an ongoing defence or control of our panic and anxiety.

Avoidance behaviour can be divided into three different categories. The first category is the avoidance of situations and/or places as an overall defence against further anxiety and panic attacks. Avoidance behaviour, either partial or total, does not necessarily mean a cessation of these, but for many of us it can mean relative safety and, most importantly, privacy.

We become restricted in where we can and can't go. We may find we can travel within a certain radius of a few kilometres of home, and do everything we normally do in relative comfort and safety. Once outside this invisible boundary our anxiety soars. As an overall control of the disorder we stay within certain boundaries. This may mean becoming restricted not only to the house, but to one room. But even then the anxiety and panic attacks can still remain.

Our avoidance behaviour can also be very subtle and gradual, as our area of relative 'safety' diminishes over time. We are able to do some things one day, only to find ourselves unable to do them the next. Although it appears illogical to others, this defence against panic attacks and anxiety can mean a possible reduction in them. The cost of this defence is high, as it can mean a total breakdown of our previous lifestyle.

ANTICIPATORY ANXIETY

The second category of avoidance behaviour is caused by anticipatory anxiety, the 'what ifs'. This category differs from the first in its defence and control. The first category is an overall, ongoing attempt to control the disorder, the second is a defence against a specific spiral of high anxiety.

Anticipatory anxiety is the fear of having a panic attack while meeting a specific commitment. The overall defence against ongoing anxiety and panic attacks sometimes reduces them to a manageable level. However, the relative safety is lost when we have to break through our invisible boundaries to meet a specific commitment. It can be going to the local shop, going out with family or friends, or anything.

It doesn't matter if the event is five minutes or five months away. The anticipation of having to go beyond our invisible boundaries means breaking our tenuous control of our overall defence. This triggers the 'what ifs'—'What if I can't do it?' 'What if I do have a panic attack?' By the time we need to leave home to meet the commitment, our anxiety level may be so high that we cancel our plans and stay at home. In other words, we avoid the commitment because of a specific spiral of anxiety.

FEELING UNWELL

The third category of avoidance behaviour is scarcely recognised by anyone who does not have the disorder. It is the avoidance of situations and/or places by feeling generally unwell most of the time. Some people compare this to ongoing flu-like symptoms. We are also continually exhausted, as the anxiety and panic attacks consume all our energy. Going out, going to work or doing the normal day-to-day things around the house means not only trying to keep the anxiety and panic attacks at bay, but also trying to overcome the feeling of being unwell and the all-consuming fatigue.

Alcohol

The use of alcohol is another form of control and some people will go on to develop an alcohol dependence. Lack of diagnosis and/or effective treatment has meant some people have used alcohol as a way of 'self-medication'. This was often the case in our parents' and grandparents' generations where an anxiety disorder could be 'hidden' behind what was perceived as primarily an alcohol problem.

The use of alcohol as a means of self-medication only perpetuates our panic attacks and anxiety. Most people don't recognise, or forget, that the symptoms of a hangover are very similar to the feeling state of their anxiety disorder. People misinterpret their hangover symptoms as being either their anxiety or a warning sign of an impending panic attack, and so they have another drink in an effort to control it and the cycle continues.

The stigma and shame we all feel about having an anxiety disorder can also be a factor. Quite a number of professional people have told me they feel it is more socially acceptable to admit to an alcohol problem, than to admit to having an anxiety disorder. An integral part of recovery from an anxiety disorder means that any alcohol problems need to be addressed from the outset.

Another concern is that some people use both prescribed medication and alcohol as a way of trying to control their disorder.

This can be dangerous and it is important these people speak to their doctor or psychiatrist about it.

Medication

Medication is another control that people use. In fact, it is usually the first treatment option offered. But anxiety and panic attacks can blast through the 'chemical calm' and so the dosage is increased, usually by our doctors, sometimes by ourselves. When we attempt to withdraw from the medication, our anxiety and panic attacks may return in full force as withdrawal symptoms, along with other symptoms of withdrawal. In these cases, many people revert to their normal dose of medication in an effort to stop the increased anxiety, panic attacks and symptoms of withdrawal. They become trapped in a cycle of dependence.

CASE HISTORIES

Patricia

The prescription lay on the table. Would she, or wouldn't she, have it filled? Years ago Patricia had been given a similar medication. She had never liked the thought of taking it, but the panic attacks and the anxiety finally convinced her she had to do something. It had helped for a while, but over time she found she had to keep increasing the dose for it to have any effect. Finally she decided enough was enough, and slowly withdrew from the medication. Patricia had learnt to cope with the panic attacks and the anxiety, but over the last two months they had become more and more intense. She didn't want to take the medication, but as no one could suggest any other way of controlling the disorder she felt as if there were no alternative.

Robyn

Robyn looked at her mother in silence. It was no use, her mother was never going to understand that Robyn's panic disorder was a legitimate condition and that Robyn was not just being 'stupid'. Her cousin had also had panic disorder/agoraphobia and had committed suicide a month before. No one had known until after his death exactly what had been wrong with him. He had never told anyone outside his immediate family. Yet Robyn's mother still would not be convinced. She told Robyn that the family was not the type to have this sort of problem and that she had better 'pull herself together' and stop being so ridiculous.

Self-absorption

Although self-absorption is not a secondary condition it is another control that many of us use, often without realising it. Our self-absorption will seem to family and friends that we are continually dwelling on our disorder. We are, but not in the way it appears. There is much truth in the statement that 'dwelling on something only makes it worse'. With an anxiety disorder, not dwelling on it is almost impossible. We feel as if our lives or our sanity are in constant danger. We feel we may lose control or embarrass ourselves in some way and so it is extremely difficult not to think about it.

What we don't realise is, the more we think about it, the more we worry about it, the harder we try to control it, the worse we get. Not just because we are fighting it. People who have the ability to dissociate can actually induce a trance state by becoming self-absorbed. Sometimes our absorption can be total. We can be completely focused within ourselves in a way that is very similar to meditation and, without warning, we may move into a trance state and then panic as a result. We get caught in our fearful 'what if' cycle of thinking, and round and round we go.

To understand self-absorption, we need to be aware that all people who suffer from an anxiety disorder, particularly those who are beginning to develop secondary conditions, are caught in an ever-growing maze of anxiety, panic attacks and fear. There appears to be nothing that we or anyone can do to stop it. The results of this are totally devastating. Under the circumstances it is completely normal and natural to become preoccupied. In fact, not to be preoccupied would be abnormal. The absorption is an attempt to find a way out of our distress. Essentially, we are trying to find answers to what appear to be unanswerable questions.

Our absorption is also part of the monitoring process. Monitoring each symptom is another way we try to defend ourselves against them. If we know what our symptoms 'are doing' we feel we won't be taken by surprise in the next minute or the next hour. This is part of our 'early warning' system against further panic attacks and against the big one we feel sure is circling waiting to strike!

The need to be in control

There is a final control that actually forms the basis of all the other controls we use. It can be so subtle that many of us may not be aware of it. It is the need to be in control, not only of ourselves but of our whole environment. The need to be in control permeates every aspect of our life. With the development of our anxiety disorder, we feel we need to fight harder to be in control as we have already lost so much to the disorder, and we are so afraid of losing control altogether.

Most of us have never been aware of our need to be in control, but it has always been part of us long before the onset of our disorder. As a result of our disorder, our need to be in control becomes paramount. Our sense of helplessness and fear demands nothing less. When the anxiety and panic attacks break away from this control we feel even more helpless than before.

The need to be in control is one of the main obstacles to recovery. Recovery means the opposite. Recovery means we need to let go of the need to be in control. We don't realise that our overwhelming need to be in control perpetuates our disorder. Once we can let go of this particular control, we gain control over our panic and anxiety.

There are various aspects to this particular control, which I discuss in detail later. To let go of this control is unimaginable, but letting go means recovery, and with recovery comes freedom.

CHAPTER 4

THERAPIES

Many people have tried a number of therapies and treatments with little or no effective outcome. Not only does this contribute to a general sense of helplessness and hopelessness, it also generates anger towards the health professions.

We may be angry about the overall lack of understanding and knowledge of anxiety disorders, or at not receiving an earlier diagnosis and effective treatment. Many people who have had the disorder for years feel cheated by the loss of family, social and employment opportunities. There is also anger that doctors' failure to understand has strengthened the myths and stigma surrounding anxiety disorders. These myths suggest we are weak in character, not trying hard enough, or gaining too many secondary benefits from the disorder to really want to recover.

Now there are effective treatment options available we can use our anger constructively by becoming more proactive. It is up to us as individuals to access as much information as we can about the various treatment options and to choose the most effective option/s to meet our needs. Our recovery demands nothing less.

We can also become more proactive in our choice of doctor or therapist. Many of us accept inadequate treatment because we think we are inadequate. We don't think we have the right to change doctors or voice our concerns, and then we become angry because we don't receive the help we need.

In some cases there can be misguided loyalty to doctor, therapist or family. Although we complain privately, we continue to go back to our doctor or therapist because we feel we don't want to let our family, doctor or therapist down. In some cases family members feel a stronger loyalty to the therapist than we do. The family pressures us to remain with the therapist, so we stay in a therapy situation which may be of little benefit.

The need to be perfect

Before the anxiety disorder many of us were perfectionists and, despite the current disorder, many of us still try to present this image. Not only have we tried to be the perfect partner, the perfect parent, the perfect employee or employer, but we become the perfect patient. Discussing issues where we feel ashamed or humiliated does not fit our 'perfect' image, so we hold back.

I have seen this happen on so many occasions. In many instances we do not tell our doctor or therapist the full effects of what we are experiencing, including thoughts of suicide. I have even seen people discharged from treatment because they present the perfect image to their therapist. 'They are going well and have their disorder under control'—yet they may be in more difficulty than when they first started treatment. The last thing we need, and the last thing our therapists need, is a perfect patient!

Treatment

Many of us go from one therapy to another, only to find ourselves back where we started. Although the panic attacks and anxiety may diminish for a while, they come back, sometimes worse than before.

Irrespective of how many therapies we have tried, the overall lack of understanding means that most of us have never been taught how to manage our disorder ourselves. Few treatments teach management skills, and many only treat one particular aspect of the disorder. The disorder and its secondary conditions need to be treated as a whole, not in isolation to each other.

It is important for all of us to understand that, although various therapies may not have worked by themselves, when they are used in conjunction they can become extremely powerful tools for recovery. We may need one treatment option at one stage of the recovery process, and a different one at another stage. We need to choose what is right for us and what is appropriate to our needs at each stage of the recovery process.

Medication

Medication is usually the 'front-line' defence against panic attacks and anxiety. Most people don't want to take medication but in the majority of cases it is the only form of treatment offered. While there is a time and place for medication, especially if someone is feeling suicidal, medication by itself is not a long-term answer for many people. If we do accept medication, we have a responsibility to ourselves to become proactive and informed about it.

We can feel embarrassed and ashamed or may feel we have no right to ask questions or raise the concerns we have about the medication being prescribed. This is quite wrong. We have every right to ask and most doctors and psychiatrists are more than willing to answer questions and discuss any concerns.

We need to know the expected short-term and long-term outcomes, how long we will be taking the medication and how long it takes for the medication to begin to work. For example, it may take four to six weeks for the full effects of an antidepressant to be felt.

We also need to know about possible side effects and possible withdrawal symptoms or 'discontinuation' reactions (BMJ 1998). Sometimes, people are told their medication has no side effects and/or no potential withdrawal or discontinuation symptoms. We need to check this information for ourselves. We can change doctors or speak with our local pharmacist or access a number of websites that provide this information.

We should check for potential interactions with other medications, including herbal and other over-the-counter preparations, and any interactions with alcohol. Women considering pregnancy or breast-feeding need to know of any possible risk to the baby. When we have this information we can make a responsible decision in conjunction with our doctor or therapist as to the most suitable treatment for us.

When we begin to use medication we may sometimes experience side effects. This is not always the case but, if it is, then we do need to speak to our doctor about it. Depending on the side effects and their severity, the doctor may wish us to continue with it or may change the medication.

Occasionally, some people are told it is their anxiety, not the medication, that is creating the new symptoms. It is then up to us either to seek a second opinion or to check out possible side effects of the medication ourselves, as described above.

Sometimes people can take medication for months or years with little effect. If there is no marked change in our anxiety disorder after being on medication for eight weeks, then we do need to discuss this with our doctor and ask for the medication to be changed. If we are refused, we need to change doctors!

If we are told we will need to be on medication for the rest of our life, we do need to ask why and seek a referral to a cognitive behavioural therapist. Again, if we are refused, we do need to change doctors. This also applies if we are told we need to be on medication for a year or two before seeing a CB therapist. Again we need to ask why and then, depending on the answer, we can seek a second opinion.

Many people become frustrated because they only see their doctor or psychiatrist for ten to fifteen minutes every few weeks to have their prescription renewed. Again, we need to ask for a referral to a CB therapist and, if refused, we need to change doctors.

Some people report that their doctor or psychiatrist doesn't recommend CBT or they are told it is ineffective in the treatment of anxiety disorders. This is another instance where we do need to consider changing therapists as CBT is considered a 'best practice' in the treatment of anxiety disorders.

It is extremely important that we do not skip or forget to take our medication at the prescribed times. Some people may begin to experience withdrawal or discontinuation reactions by missing just one dose. Another equally important point is that we must not just stop taking our medication as this can be dangerous. If we do want to stop using it we need to speak to our doctor and withdraw slowly under medical supervision.

TRANQUILLISERS

Tranquillisers were one of the first defences against anxiety and panic. Research shows these drugs can be addictive. While there can be a role for tranquillisers, especially in helping to ease any crisis that people may experience at the beginning of their disorder, the guideline is to prescribe tranquillisers for two to four weeks only (Brayley et al. 1991). This minimises the risk of addiction.

Many people are still being prescribed tranquillisers on a long-term basis. If they are using one of the shorter-acting tranquillisers, withdrawal symptoms can occur if they do not take their medication at the prescribed time. These withdrawal symptoms can include anxiety and panic attacks. Sometimes these symptoms are attributed to the original disorder and the dosage of medication is actually increased, leading to further dependency on the medication.

Unfortunately, in some instances people are still being told that tranquillisers are either not addictive, or that the latest research shows they are not as addictive as first thought. It is difficult and confusing when we are confronted with these conflicting points of view, but we have a responsibility to ourselves to become informed and then to make the decision about whether to use tranquillisers in the long term.

Part of the recovery process for people using tranquillisers means slowly withdrawing the medication under supervision of their doctor or psychiatrist. Research suggests that CBT can be very effective during withdrawal (Otto et al. 1994) and it can help us to work through this process effectively.

ANTIDEPRESSANTS

Antidepressants are now widely used in the treatment of anxiety disorders, with varying degrees of success in keeping the anxiety and the panic attacks at bay. While antidepressants can be very useful if we are beginning to think about suicide, like any medication they do not teach us the cognitive skills we need. If we decide to use an antidepressant we can use the time while taking them to learn personal management skills. These skills will enable us to control any future panic attacks and anxiety ourselves once we have withdrawn from the medication.

Research now confirms the possibility that some people may develop 'discontinuation reactions' as they withdraw their antidepressant. These reactions can begin within a short time after the medication has been withdrawn and can last for 'one day to three weeks' (BMJ 1998). As the discontinuation reactions can include anxiety and panic attacks, it is important the reaction is not misinterpreted by ourselves or our therapist as being a return of our anxiety disorder. This could lead 'to unnecessary reinstatement of the antidepressant' (BMJ 1998).

Cognitive behavioural skills will help us if we do experience any of these discontinuation reactions, and they will also help us to control any future panic attacks or anxiety.

Cognitive behavioural therapy (CBT)

When medication is used it does need to be used in conjunction with other therapies. We control every aspect of our life except the way we think, yet it is our thinking that is the major contributor to the perpetuation of our anxiety disorder.

Many of us are aware of the predominant role played by our thoughts. This was confirmed in one Australian study of panic disorder which showed that patients had 'a clear bias toward attributing cause to cognitive factors' (Kenardy et al. 1988). As in my experience with clients, the study also showed that people preferred 'cognitive coping strategies' in preference to medication (Kenardy et al. 1988).

We continually add to our fear by the way we think. In other words, we are continually frightening ourselves with our thoughts.

CBT is a series of strategies specifically targeted to our particular disorder. For panic disorder these strategies can include relaxation, breathing techniques, 'interoceptive exposure', exposure to situations and places we have been avoiding and cognitive therapy. *Interoceptive exposure* is designed to produce a number of the most common symptoms including accelerated heart rate, dizziness and the effects of hyperventilation. Combined with cognitive techniques we can begin to change our fearful interpretation of the symptoms and break the anxiety-producing thoughts. Armed with cognitive behavioural strategies we go into situations and/or places we have been avoiding and 'test' our ability to manage our anxiety and panic attacks.

In most cognitive programs people are instructed to write down the many thoughts that produce anxiety or panic. They are then asked to question the validity of these thoughts and to write down more realistic thoughts to counter their negative ones.

I have found that some people can become stuck with cognitive techniques in a number of ways. One way is what one of my clients calls 'analysis paralysis'. We can become stuck analysing our thoughts over and over again. If this happens, then we do need to speak with our therapist so they can assist us in breaking through the 'analysis'; otherwise, we keep going round and round in circles.

Some cognitive programs use a more 'positive thinking' approach. Most of us do become frustrated with this one. Positive thinking does not work for the majority of us at the beginning of the recovery process. If it did we would not have a problem in the first place! If we are having difficulty using a positive thinking approach it is important that we speak to our therapist about it.

Problems can also arise if we are following a cognitive program using a 'realistic' approach. This approach includes teaching people to think realistically about their panic attacks and anxiety rather than thinking they are a sign of a heart attack, or insanity or an impending loss of control. We may know and understand this at an intellectual level, but we do not believe the truth of it at an emotional level. This is the defining element in any cognitive technique. Until we can believe the truth at an emotional level we will struggle in trying to break through the wall of negativity. I discuss this further in Chapter 5.

A cognitive behavioural therapist will normally work with various types of exposure methods suited to our particular anxiety disorder. When we begin to work on our avoidance behaviour we will probably feel anxious and the 'what ifs' may return. In only a few seconds the 'what ifs' can create a mountain of fear and anxiety which seems insurmountable. We may forget the management strategies we have learnt, and become caught up in the automatic cycle of thinking. Some people will then delay doing the exposure work and wait until their anxiety disappears. This is defeating the purpose of doing exposure work! We need to go back into situations and places feeling anxious and panicky. This is how we learn to control it.

Using CBT requires commitment and discipline. If we want to learn to manage our panic attacks and anxiety ourselves then we need to be committed and do the work required, otherwise we won't recover. But it is a commitment that will give us the opportunity to break the seemingly never-ending cycle of panic and anxiety.

Graded exposure

Many people are still being given a graded exposure program only without being taught any cognitive skills. Without these skills, graded exposure is simply exposure to situations and/or places we normally avoid.

Many graded exposure programs treat the avoidance behaviour in panic disorder as though it is the situation or place that triggers the attack. People who have panic disorder without any form of avoidance behaviour are also sometimes given a graded exposure program. The question many people ask is 'exposure to what?'.

The rationale behind graded exposure programs is that when people put themselves into the situations or places they normally avoid, and stay there, the anxiety and/or panic attack will peak and slowly ebb away. In other words, the person will habituate to the anxiety and panic attack in that situation or place. But, as many people say, even though the panic attack does subside (as it always does), if they are not directly frightened of the situation or place why would the anxiety 'ebb away' when it has never done so before?

Trying to correct avoidance behaviour without working on the cause means limited success which can be destroyed by the next panic attack.

Most exposure programs insist that people stay in the situation or place until the anxiety or panic attack subsides, and this is one of the main complaints from people with panic disorder. It seems illogical to remain in a city mall, or any other place, for hours in an effort to reduce anxiety. Many people are chronically anxious, day in and day out, and are also experiencing ongoing panic attacks. As they say, if they were going to habituate to the anxiety and the panic attacks they would have already done so, irrespective of where they were.

To compound the confusion, many panic disorder clients are asked to list their secondary fears and a graded exposure program is built around them, not around the fears inherent within a spontaneous attack. In some cases the list of fears includes specific fears that predated the attacks and have no bearing on the disorder. One study showed that 'half the simple (specific) phobias in panic disorder had childhood onset and half had onset associated with the onset of panic disorder' (Argyle & Roth 1990). Yet these specific fears become incorporated into the treatment, or become the main focus of treatment. The three categories of panic attacks demonstrate quite clearly that the spontaneous panic attack is not triggered by external cues. In panic disorder, treatment needs to be directed to the cause, the spontaneous panic attack, and not the secondary fears.

CASE HISTORIES

Melissa

Melissa had a part-time job and had to work at night. On most nights she was alone, except for customers coming and going. Melissa was scared of being held up as there was always quite a bit of cash around. Her fear increased and her anxiety became all pervasive. She decided to seek help and was put on a three-month waiting list to see a therapist. During this time her anxiety and fear escalated. Melissa felt she had no alternative but to resign, but her fear and anxiety continued. When she finally saw the therapist she filled out various forms and spoke to the therapist about her fears. The next time she saw him she noticed a jar of spiders on his desk. Melissa asked him about them and he replied that, as she was also scared of spiders, the first step was to confront her fear of them. The therapist then left the office leaving her with the spiders. Melissa had always been scared of spiders, she could not remember a time when she wasn't. She didn't care about her fear of spiders, but here she was sitting in an office looking at a jar of them. All she wanted to do was to stop the anxiety so she could go back to work. She walked out and didn't go back.

Cynthia

Cynthia had panic disorder but didn't avoid anything. She went to work and did everything she had to do, but it was very difficult. She went to see a specialist although she had to wait five months for an appointment. When she got there he was three hours late. He finally arrived but didn't apologise for keeping her waiting. Although Cynthia had an hour appointment, it lasted for only twenty minutes. She told the specialist about the panic attacks and he kept asking her what she was scared of. Cynthia kept telling him she was always scared and anxious that she might die from the attacks. The specialist kept saying she had to be scared of something and Cynthia wasn't sure what he was getting at. In the end she said she had always been scared of elevators, but that was long before the panic attacks started. The specialist told her to go into the foyer and get into an elevator and go up and down in it until her anxiety disappeared. With that he finished the appointment and told her to book another with his secretary. She was so confused and angry she never went back.

Alice, Toni, Carlie

Alice asked the local discussion group about what she should do about her therapist who always went to sleep during her appointments. Toni and Carlie looked at her and told her their therapists always went to sleep too. It didn't take long for them to realise they were talking about the same therapist. When the group asked them why they didn't speak to him about it or try to find another therapist, the three of them said he was obviously very tired and they didn't want to hurt his feelings.

Psychotherapy

Psychotherapy has sometimes been the only treatment people have tried. It can be difficult to see the relevance of psychotherapy to anxiety disorders, but if we have a history of childhood abuse, or have undergone some other trauma, psychotherapy is very important. Despite the sense of shame many of us feel over these issues, they do need to be dealt with for our long-term well-being. There are very understanding and caring therapists working in the area of childhood abuse, and the local public hospital or community centre can refer anyone who needs help to these therapists.

Even if there is no major past or present trauma, psychotherapy, in conjunction with CBT, can be extremely beneficial. Many of us who have an anxiety disorder have suppressed our primary emotions of anger, grief and sadness. We don't realise they can convert to the passive feelings of anxiety and depression. Psychotherapy helps us get in touch with our emotions so we can learn to express them in healthier ways.

Some of us are frightened of psychotherapy in case we find out we are 'really bad' people. This is one of the most common fears associated with psychotherapy, but there is no basis to it. We need to take the risk. We will discover there is nothing 'bad' about us. Like everyone else, there will be aspects about ourselves we may not like but only when we know these aspects can we modify and integrate them. I discuss this further in Chapter 5.

Psychotherapy means more than just looking at the problems and difficulties of childhood. It is not so much a process of who is to blame, as a process of understanding causes and effects. It looks at how we, as children, responded in certain situations. These responses created the defences, motivations and patterns of behaviour that we unconsciously carried into adulthood, but which may not be appropriate now. When we become aware of these responses, we are then able to change them if we want to.

Hypnotherapy

Many of my clients have used hypnotherapy at some point in their disorder. While it may have helped them at that particular time, they did not fully recover and became caught up in the cycle of panic and anxiety again. Like other therapies where people are not taught the necessary cognitive skills, our panic attacks and anxiety can return, sometimes with a vengeance. If hypnosis is used, it needs to be done in conjunction with CBT.

Other therapies

A number of other treatment programs for anxiety disorders have been introduced in the last few years. One program stated that it can help people with panic disorder get over their fear of open spaces!

When considering any treatment program we need to know and verify that the program is effective and that the therapists/counsellors have a full current understanding of anxiety disorders.

Before committing to any treatment program we need to speak with the therapist/counsellor concerned. We have the right to ask them about their experience in treating people with anxiety disorders and how long they have been doing so. We also have the right to ask them for copies of their research that demonstrate the effectiveness of their treatment program. Our mental health demands nothing less!

An overview

When we look at the list of therapies it can be quite overwhelming. It isn't as daunting as it looks. Understanding of anxiety disorders has come a long way and freedom from the disorders is a reality for many of us.

CBT and medication, used together or individually, are 'best practice' in the treatment of anxiety disorders. Treatment programs which incorporate relaxation, breathing techniques and cognitive behavioural therapy have been 'associated with dramatic success' (Otto et al. 1994). A program conducted in Queensland which uses similar methods has shown 'long-term improvements'; this is not only beneficial for people with the disorder, as it 'quickly restores functioning', but is also 'cost effective' (Evans 1995). Cost is an important issue in any treatment service and cannot be ignored.

Treatment programs that do not assist us in learning how to manage our panic attacks and anxiety through cognitive techniques need to be questioned. Only we can change our thought patterns. No one can do this for us.

Recovery is a step-by-step process. While cognitive behavioural skills are the most important, short-term medication may be required. If drug or alcohol dependence is involved this will also need to be worked with. When our cognitive skills are sufficiently developed and our life is coming back on track, we may want to address any outstanding personal issues by seeing a skilled psychotherapist. The secret is to use the various therapies we need when we need them. Combined, we can take back the power.

CHAPTER 5

PRELUDE TO RECOVERY

Self-esteem

In the Tibetan Buddhist Shambhala teachings, 'the definition of bravery is not being afraid of our self' (Trungpa 1986). We are frightened of ourselves and our fear is multilayered. At the top level is our anxiety disorder and beneath it is the fear of our self. This fear is the reason we have not developed a strong, healthy sense of self-esteem, and this in turn has paved the way for the triggering of our anxiety disorder.

Healthy self-esteem and anxiety disorders are mutually exclusive. A healthy sense of self-esteem comes from a strong sense of authenticity within one's self. A sense of 'who I am'.

From this vantage point our perception is clearer and more expansive. We know and understand ourselves, we are able to deal with the variety of stress that comes our way without violating or negating ourselves. We are able to understand our own minds with more clarity, we are able to see choices in everything we think and do. We are able to honour and respect ourselves by taking responsibility for those choices and for their outcomes.

There has been very little recognition of the role of self-esteem, or lack of it, in the development of our anxiety disorder. There is also little recognition of the role that self-esteem plays during the recovery process from our disorder. Yet it becomes the definitive answer to permanent recovery.

Panic and anxiety management skills allow us to control our anxiety and attacks, but if our lack of self-esteem is not addressed it can become the catalyst for possible future incidents of our disorder. Healthy self-esteem is the ultimate prevention strategy.

When I ask the question 'Who am I?' in the workshops I facilitate, the answer revolves around what people do: I am a mother, a father, a wife, a husband, a daughter, a son, a sister, a brother, a friend, a school teacher, a nurse, an engineer, a computer programmer, a receptionist, a cabinet maker, a shop assistant, a student. We identity ourselves by the various roles we play and we are identified with these roles by other people. Yet the roles we play don't answer the question of who I am.

When we first develop an anxiety disorder our catch-cry is, 'This is not me. I am not like this.' When we say, 'This is not me', we are referring to the image we had of ourselves before we developed the disorder. This is reinforced by other people when we tell them we have a disorder: 'Not you! You can't have. You're such a strong person.'

There is no doubt that we are the strong ones in the family. We are the one everyone turns to with their problems. We take care of everyone's feelings, we go out of our way not to hurt them, even if this means we are hurting ourselves. We feel guilty about almost everything: 'I should have done this. I shouldn't have done that.' 'Why did I say this, why did I say that?' 'What if they take what I said the wrong way?'

We try to be the perfect partner, parent, sibling, daughter, son, friend, employee, employer, acquaintance. If we don't get it just right, if things don't work out the way we think they should, we just keep on trying harder and harder. We can spend our life trying a bit harder than we did last week, last month, last year. We think that, if we just try a little bit harder in everything we do, we can finally become this ideal person we think we should be. One who is everything to everybody, who loves unconditionally, who is whole, healthy, happy, secure, content and at peace with themselves . . . if we just try a little harder.

If we look beyond our identity and our behaviours to answer the question of 'Who am I?' what do we find? We find confusion, pain, conflict, self-contempt, a sense of emptiness and loneliness. This is reflected in our lack of confidence, lack of self-esteem, and our feelings of inadequacy and is reflected in our inability to break through and take charge of our lives. In short, we find a lack of a sense of self, a lack of connection to our self. It all sounds quite dramatic, doesn't it? However, the implications and impact of our lack of connection to our self is dramatic.

What will other people think?

In trying so hard to be who we think we should be, we have denied and totally invalidated ourselves. We came to believe from a very early age that in order to be liked, accepted or loved we needed to conform to the needs and expectations of others. In doing so, we rejected our self and continue to do so every day of our lives. This is the conflict. Many of us who have now recovered see our anxiety, panic attacks and depression as being an anguished call from our self demanding its rightful acknowledgement and validation in all aspects of our lives.

'What will other people think?' becomes the motivation for our behaviour and our actions. In almost all we do, we take mental stock before, during and after each encounter. It takes so much hard work to estimate the needs of others, especially when those needs are hard to define, so we are always on duty to make sure we have not upset anyone, offended anyone, caused anyone any grief. However brief the encounter, the impression we have to try to make is at least a good one, if not a perfect one. In the process we lose our connection to self and along with it the ability to recognise and address our own needs and wants, especially if these are in contradiction to what we feel other people expect from us.

'What will other people think?' inhibits our ability to feel and express our own emotions fully, to live our life creatively and to our full potential. This can be threatening to us, because other people may not appreciate these qualities. And if they don't appreciate them, they may not think well of us. If they don't think well of us, then who are we?

'What will people think?' is the cause. The lack of a sense of self and ensuing lack of self-esteem is the effect. We take on the responsibility for living our lives in accordance with what we perceive others will value in us, and unknowingly we give away our feeling of connection to our self and our personal power. This in turn generates the dislike or hatred we feel towards ourselves and fuels our feelings of emptiness, loneliness and confusion about who we really are. And the question is: How did we as intelligent adults end up like this?

'What will people think?' 'They may not like me, may not love me.' 'If they don't care for me, then what do I do?' 'What would happen to me?' Irrespective of our childhood backgrounds, whether they have been abusive or not, these are the perceptions and fears we have all carried with us since childhood.

The need to be liked or loved is universal and an inherent part of being human. However, as adults, we are still perceiving this need through the eyes of the child we once were. We have matured intellectually, we have matured physically, but we have not matured emotionally. We have held our emotional development back for fear of what other people would think and this has major ramifications in the development, and in the recovery process, of our anxiety disorder.

Emotions

While we are not our emotions, our emotions are part of who we are. Irrespective of our childhood backgrounds, we all learnt that the expression of our emotions was 'bad'. That we continued to feel them meant we were bad. People don't love or like bad people. I am aware this can be perceived as incredibly simplistic, but our childhood impressions of our self and our emotions created a complex myriad of effects. It is the unweaving of these complexities that exposes the root fear.

I use the word 'bad' deliberately. As we pursue the question of 'Who am I?' in my workshops, the bottom line is always the same. People are frightened of finding out, or of even beginning to explore, who they are in case they discover that they are in fact a 'bad' person. The fear of being or becoming a bad person is the major fear we have always had, even prior to our anxiety disorder. This fear is so widespread it cuts across all socioeconomic groups and childhood backgrounds, abusive or non-abusive. Why do so many people fear they are 'bad' or will become a 'bad' person?

How often do we use the word 'bad'? It is such a small word and we use it so freely. We say it to our pets: 'Bad dog', 'bad cat'. How often do we use the word 'bad' when chastising our children? How many times were we told by our parents that we were bad ? Yet we would rarely use this word in the context of an adult.

What happened when we were children and we became angry? We soon learned that any expression of our anger was bad even though other people could express theirs towards us! We learned that being angry put us at risk in one way or another. Being angry also meant we risked losing people's love, irrespective of the form this love took.

Our anger was a threat to us and so we needed to deal with it in another way. We learned to block it out of our awareness, sometimes to the degree that some of us don't ever feel our own anger. If we do feel it, we usually turn it back on ourselves with our ever present internal critic: 'I'm stupid, I'm hopeless, useless, dumb.'

We also learned to turn off our feelings of grief and sadness. Men, and many eldest daughters, were taught not to cry. Men don't cry.

They have to be tough. Eldest daughters don't cry. They should be looking after their younger siblings. As with our anger, we learned from other people's verbal and non-verbal behaviours that our feelings of sadness or grief were not acceptable. Like our anger, we repressed them.

Our creativity, our sense of adventure, our curiosity, our spontaneity, our joyfulness—again, the messages we received told us these were inappropriate. 'Act your age!' 'Grow up!' 'Don't be childish.' The verbal and non-verbal behaviour of others confirmed our thoughts that other people may not like or love us if we acted in any of these ways, so, as with our anger and sadness, we turned them off.

Other rebukes and messages we received were also interpreted by us as a threat to the love/caring we needed. If we did not share, if we did not care for others, if we took time out for ourselves, we were being selfish. Again we learned this was not appropriate behaviour and we learned to take care of others and neglected to take care of ourselves. Even now, the question of what selfishness means permeates our life and can become one of the initial stumbling blocks of the recovery process. Many of us feel that taking time out for ourselves or caring for ourselves is selfish and unacceptable. It is not who we should be.

As children we created a self based upon an 'ideal' model of who we thought we needed to be and we have been chasing this ideal ever since. By doing so we rejected and denied not only our self, but also our emotional development.

Emotional development

This denial of self creates numerous effects. Two of the most important effects, in relation to our anxiety disorder, are our passivity and our need to be in control. We are extremely passive people. We have needed to be so, as this is part of our ideal model and ensures we don't express our emotions. We remain passive despite the onslaught of an anxiety disorder that can destroy our life as we knew it. We don't realise that being angry at our disorder is a natural and normal response to the devastation of our lives. Any anger we may feel towards our panic and anxiety is turned back on ourselves. 'I'm stupid, hopeless, useless.' Anger directed at our disorder can be the rocket-ship to recovery, yet many people are afraid of becoming angry, even towards their panic and anxiety. They feel it is a loss of control rather than a major step forward in their recovery.

To be who we think we should be takes an enormous amount of self-control. We have needed to be in control of ourselves, our emotions and our environment at all times to ensure that the image other people have of us is not diminished. This self-control is not what it appears to be (see Chapter 3). It is the 'glue' that holds the created self together, and keeps our natural emotions and feelings at bay.

When anxiety and panic attacks blast into our lives we are thrown back onto ourselves. No matter how hard we try to fight and control our anxiety and panic, we can't break through. Our panic and anxiety escalate along with our fears and a growing sense of inadequacy and increasing helplessness. The more we fight for control, the more helpless and isolated we feel, and our anxiety and attacks gain momentum.

In becoming who we thought 'we should be' we have blocked our emotional development. We are still relating emotionally to ourselves and the world around us as we did as a child. It is within this framework that we relate to our anxiety disorder. This is why it has power over us.

Intellectually, we have matured and, intellectually, we may know and understand that our symptoms are those of anxiety and panic. Intellectually, we know there is nothing physically wrong with us. Intellectually, we know our thoughts are creating our ongoing distress. Emotionally, we do not feel the truth of this and, emotionally, we do not believe it.

We don't believe that we will not die or go insane from our anxiety and panic symptoms. We don't believe we will not lose control, make a fool of ourselves or embarrass ourselves in some way. Emotionally, we do not feel the truth of the countless positive statements and affirmations that we repeat endlessly, or the realistic statements we say to counteract negative thoughts.

Emotionally, we sabotage our intellectual understanding of our disorder and we become caught in a never-ending cycle of fear. In dealing with fear, we are dealing with emotions and no amount of intellectual dissection will bring the two levels together without further understanding.

I speak about recovery as a *change of perception*. We need to bring our emotional understanding of our disorder to the same level as our intellectual understanding. Emotionally, we need to learn to see and feel our panic attacks and anxiety for what they really are—panic and anxiety, nothing more. This does not negate the severity and strength of them. They will still feel as violent as before but, emotionally, we can learn to see and feel why there is nothing to fear. Until we can see this, we are a prisoner of our fear.

Recovery is the loss of fear of our experience. When we can see and feel our intellectual understanding at an emotional level, our symptoms and fears lose their power over us. We then have power over them.

The practice of mindfulness facilitates this integration (see Chapter 9). When we first begin, it appears to be an intellectual exercise going nowhere. Initially, there is no connection between the 'head' and the 'heart', the intellectual and the emotional. With practice, we begin to understand at an emotional level the dynamics of our anxiety disorder. We begin to 'see' and feel, at an emotional level, how our thoughts create so much of our ongoing distress, which in turn creates the many fears we experience. We begin to see the subtle and not so subtle physical effects of our thoughts. We begin to see the mind/body connection very clearly. And as we do, our emotional understanding of our disorder develops, and the 'power' balance between ourselves and our anxiety disorder begins to shift. Our panic and anxiety become easier and easier to manage and control, and we begin to reclaim our lives.

We all assume recovery will mean going back to who we were before our disorder. This isn't recovery. How can it be if it involves 'going back'? Going back means we do not lose the fear of our experience. Recovery means we go forward, not backwards. If we go back, we remain at the level of emotional development we had before the disorder developed. This sets the stage for a possible recurrence of our disorder in the future.

As we work through to recovery our emotional development evolves as part of this process. As it does, we begin to see how the inherent negativity of our disorder can actually be transformed into the most constructive experience of our life. This becomes the gift of recovery. This is the reason why those of us who have recovered consider our anxiety disorder to be the most valuable experience of our life.

As the recovery process gains momentum our panic and anxiety become our teachers. The more mindful we become, the more we see how much of our anxiety is being created by trying to be who we think we should be. Our anxiety teaches us when we are not being true to ourselves, when we are denying or invalidating ourselves in some way.

One classic example of how we repress our own needs occurs when we say 'yes' to doing something for someone when we actually want to say 'no'. We smile, say 'yes' and immediately think, 'Why do I have to do this? Why is it always me?' We feel angry at ourselves and resentful toward the other person. We then think 'Why am I so selfish?' and feel guilty for feeling this way; and so our anxiety is generated.

Not only have we repressed our own need to say 'no'—by saying 'yes' we have also betrayed our responsibility and integrity to our self. In doing so, we have taken responsibility for the other person plus we are not being honest with them.

The more we become aware, the more we see the choices we have in any given situation. The more we choose to honour and respect our own needs and feelings, the less anxiety and panic we feel.

This becomes the process of working through, not just to recovery but also to the development of a healthy sense of self with its inherent self-esteem. And the answer to the question of 'Who am I?'

PART 2

FIVE STEPS TO
FREEDOM
· A N D ·
POWER

CHAPTER 6

STEPS 1 & 2 UNDERSTANDING AND ACCEPTANCE

The development of an anxiety disorder can destroy our lives. We can live with the power of the disorder for many years and, no matter what we do, we feel completely powerless. But we are not. We can take back the power!

Recovery for many of us who had panic disorder means we may still experience an occasional attack if we are tired or extremely stressed. The difference between panic disorder and recovery means we have lost all fear of our attacks. Once we lose the fear we lose the disorder and the anxiety over our attacks. There are no more 'what ifs'; instead we have developed an attitude of 'So what?', irrespective of how violent the occasional attack may feel. Feeling and believing 'So what?' is the power.

Kindness and compassion

One of the first obstacles to recovery is the lack of compassion we have for ourselves. Compassion in this instance is the capacity to feel our own suffering without mentally abusing ourselves—'I am hopeless, stupid, worthless'—and without the brutal self-hatred many of us feel. We won't be able to develop any sense of personal power while we negate ourselves in this way.

In the early stages of the disorder many of us say, 'This is not me, I am not like this. I shouldn't be feeling this. I should be able to get my act together.' In doing so we negate, deny and invalidate our own suffering by mentally abusing ourselves.

Recovery demands that we learn to be compassionate toward ourselves. We need to begin to be kind to ourselves in the same way as we care about, and feel compassion for, other people who are experiencing an anxiety disorder. Only when we begin to care about, and be kind to, our self can we begin to take back the power. Understanding why we have developed an anxiety disorder is the first step in recovery and the first step to developing a more compassionate attitude towards our self.

Stress

Everyone experiences stress, and everyone reacts in different ways when they reach their individual threshold to stress. The fact that we have reached ours does not mean we are weak, it means we are human. Not super-human, as we think we should be. Some people develop high blood pressure, others a migraine. When we reach the limit of our threshold to stress we experience a panic attack. Our lack of understanding and our reactions of fear and anxiety place us under further stress, and the vicious circle begins.

Anxiety disorders are not life-threatening in themselves. It is only our lack of understanding that makes them appear so.

Understanding is the first step in taking back the power and in working toward recovery. Recovery is a step-by-step process. If we have been diagnosed as having a panic-related anxiety disorder, the first step is to understand the disorder fully and accept the diagnosis.

The fight-and-flight response

The fight-and-flight response is an automatic response within the body which is activated when we are in danger, or perceive ourselves to be in danger. Stress hormones including adrenalin are released into the bloodstream to prepare us either to flee the situation or to stay and confront it.

Irrespective of which disorder we have, it is our thoughts that create the 'danger' and our fear that activates the fight-and-flight response, which we feel as symptoms of anxiety and panic. These symptoms add to our fear which keeps the fight-and-flight response activated and we become trapped in an ongoing cycle.

This is why *loss of fear* is so important. Losing our fear, whether it is the fear of having a panic attack or one of the other fears specific to the other anxiety disorders, is central to our long-term recovery. Initially, it is difficult because we do not have the overall understanding of why our symptoms and fears will not hurt us. We need to understand why we are not going to die, go insane or lose control in some way through our anxiety disorder.

Fear of death

RAPID HEARTBEAT

The most common fear in panic disorder is that we will die from a heart attack. The experience of a rapid heartbeat, or palpitations, or 'missed' heartbeats seems to confirm our fear there is something wrong with our heart. What we don't realise is that these symptoms are effects of the fight-and-flight response. Our heart rate does increase when the response is activated. It is part of the body's preparation either to run from the dangerous situation or to stay and fight it.

Many people unknowingly aggravate these particular symptoms by continually monitoring their pulse. The thought 'What's my heart rate?' can turn on the fight-and-flight response. As they take their pulse, they find their heart rate has increased, 'confirming' their fears that there is something 'definitely' wrong with their heart. Yet it was simply the thought that triggered the fight-and-flight response.

Once our doctor confirms that our symptoms are part of our anxiety and panic, and not a sign that something is wrong with our heart, then we need to believe the doctor. If not, we will continue to think about it, which turns on the fight-and-flight response, and around we go!

MUSCLE TENSION

The fear of having a heart attack is compounded by the tightness or pain that we may experience in the chest, the left arm and, sometimes, the jaw. Most people know these can be signs of a heart attack, but with anxiety disorders they are a sign that the fight-and-flight response is activated. Our muscles tense in preparation for us either to fight or flee. We may also feel this tension in the neck and head and as a tightness or constriction in the throat. It can feel as if we are choking or are unable to breathe. Once we have learnt to control our thoughts, the muscle tension disappears along with our racing heart.

BREATHING DIFFICULTIES

Our rapid, shallow breathing is also caused by the fight-and-flight response. Some people become so frightened by their shallow breathing they feel as if their breathing will stop completely. In other instances, people feel they can't take a deep breath because of the tightness in their chest.

Over-breathing is known as hyperventilation, and its symptoms are similar to those of an attack. There was a theory that hyperventilation was the actual cause of panic attacks but it is now accepted that, while hyperventilation can be experienced as part of the overall symptoms, it is not the cause.

The symptoms of hyperventilation include pins and needles, feeling light-headed or dizzy and feeling as if we may faint. When we hyperventilate we become even more frightened which, in turn, keeps the fight-and-flight response going and the cycle continues.

I meet very few people who have actually fainted. A small number of people have told me they have occasionally fallen to the floor, but even then they have never lost consciousness. Even if it does happen there is nothing to be alarmed about. Fainting can be seen as the body's way of getting 'us' with our fearful thinking, out of its way so that our breathing can be returned to normal. It is important to add that if we haven't yet fainted or fallen to the floor as a result of our anxiety and panic then we probably never will. If it were going to happen it would have been during the initial stages of the disorder.

The effects of hyperventilation can be alleviated quite easily by breathing very slowly and deeply.

Another simple and effective way to stop these symptoms is to cup our hands over our mouth and nose and breathe into them. This method is a variation on the most common technique of easing hyperventilation—breathing into a paper bag. But I can't help wondering about this method—we are all frightened of what other people will think of us and pulling out a paper bag and breathing into it in the office or shopping centre would probably cause us to hyperventilate further!

With so many symptoms involving the heart and breathing, it is only natural to be afraid that we may die. Understanding why we have these symptoms, and understanding why they won't hurt us, will help us to lose the fear. When we lose the fear we turn off the fight-and-flight response and the symptoms ease.

When we are assured by our doctor that there is nothing wrong we need to accept it. Our recovery depends on it. If we don't accept it, we will continue to be afraid and our fear will continually activate the fight-and-flight response. If we still doubt the diagnosis or have any new symptoms then we need to speak to our doctor again.

Fear of insanity

The fear of insanity is the second most common fear. Trying to understand what is happening to us continually pushes us to the limits of our knowledge. We cannot find anything in our past experience that even comes close to what we are experiencing now, so many of us feel we are going insane.

We're not, although it often feels like it. Some of the other symptoms we experience don't help to break this fear—they usually add to it. Our experience of depersonalisation or derealisation or other dissociative symptoms can feel as if we are going insane. We aren't!

Our fear of insanity can be compounded if we experience a lack of concentration, one of the effects of an anxiety disorder. Our concentration can be severely affected to the point where we are unable to concentrate on the most simple things. Yet our concentration is not diminished. Rather it is internally directed instead of externally directed. As I said in Chapter 3, many of us do become very self-absorbed. We may try to concentrate on everyday tasks but, unknowingly, we continually draw back our concentration so that it is internally directed.

Another effect of our anxiety disorder can be the loss of all feelings we have towards people who are close to us, our partners, family and friends. This can be particularly distressing and again adds to our fear that we are going insane. We don't actually 'lose' our feelings—they become lost in the confusion and fear that we feel. If we think we are going to die, go insane or lose control in some way, we feel as if we are fighting for our survival. There is not a lot of time or energy left to be directed elsewhere.

This also applies to the loss of libido. While this can be a side effect of antidepressants, people who are not taking these drugs can also experience it. But as I said above, we simply don't have the energy for anything else! As we begin to lose our fear of our panic and anxiety our feelings and libido do return.

Fear of losing control

This is the third most common fear. Our lack of understanding of the disorder accentuates this fear. We feel so much has already happened that we haven't been able to control, and every day seems to bring with it new symptoms and new fears. We can't help but feel the time will come when we will lose control completely.

We can feel as if we may lose control of our bowel or bladder, or that we will be sick. Nausea can become our constant companion, and if we look at all our symptoms it is no wonder. Our body does feel as if it is out of control. When we imagine these events happening we also imagine our embarrassment and humiliation. Naturally, this only increases the fear.

Again, I rarely meet anyone who has had these fears realised, although people speak of their 'close calls'. The feeling that we may lose control of bowel or bladder, and the nausea we feel, are effects of the fight-and-flight response. Once we are practising a cognitive technique we stop the response from being activated.

Feeling faint

The sensation of feeling faint and/or dizzy can be a result of not eating, dissociation, hyperventilation, or a combination of all three. The nausea that many people feel with their anxiety disorder can result in feeling too sick to eat. I don't mean occasionally missing meals, but simply not eating. Lack of food will cause feelings of faintness or dizziness, shaking and an overall sense of weakness.

We forget these sensations are a natural result of not eating and put them down to anxiety, which in turn adds to the cycle. Not eating can also make those of us who do dissociate more vulnerable to dissociation. Attention to our diet is extremely important. If we do have difficulty eating it is advisable to ask our doctor for assistance.

We also need to become aware of whether our feelings of dizziness or faintness are actually a result of dissociation. We can feel dizzy when we dissociate. It is not so much the trace state that causes this, but rather the magnitude of the change in consciousness (Fewtrell & O'Connor 1988). For those of us who do dissociate, once we become more aware of our ability to do this we will be able to develop greater control over it.

We can also feel faint as a result of hyperventilating. If so, we do need to adjust our breathing.

COMPLETE LOSS OF CONTROL

This fear can be terrifying. People interpret it to mean they may act uncontrollably and hurt themselves or others. They don't.

The fear of losing control completely comes from the loss of control we have already experienced. The harder we fight to get control, the more we lose control. Not over ourselves, but over our life.

We do not lose control of ourselves through our anxiety disorder. If this was going to happen it would have happened from the very beginning. It will not happen now or in the future.

Ironically, recovery means letting go of the control we are fighting so hard to maintain, 'fighting' being the operative word. 'Fighting' turns on the fight-and-flight response. Once we can let go of this need for control we actually gain control over our disorder. The concept of letting go can be very frighting for people when they read or hear about it for the first time and I will be discussing this in the coming chapters.

Acceptance

Understanding our disorder is the first step in taking back the power. Acceptance is the second step. When we are diagnosed as having an anxiety disorder we need to accept it, otherwise we will not be able to recover. We can't recover from something if we don't believe we have it in the first place!

The starting point is to accept: 'This is me and I have an anxiety disorder.' We need to accept the disorder and ourselves totally, not with fear and not with shame or humiliation, but with understanding and compassion. When we can fully accept ourselves as we are at the moment, we can begin to work towards the future when we won't have an anxiety disorder.

There are various stages to full acceptance. Even when we have accepted we have an anxiety disorder it can still dominate our life. Through our fear we remain passive towards it. And many of our fears show that we actually don't accept it as much as we may think, because our fears still revolve around the fear of dying, going insane or losing control. If we fully accepted our disorder we would be able to be more proactive in our approach to it, rather than remaining passive towards it.

If we feel angry or frustrated with our disorder we turn it around and take it out on ourselves. 'I'm stupid, hopeless, a failure.' Why? Why aren't we angry at the disorder? It can dominate our life. We need to take back the power. We need to dominate it. Everyone wants to recover, but we need to reach a point where enough is enough. Used constructively, the power of our anger and frustration can motivate us to develop an attitude of 'I will recover no matter what!' This is full acceptance. We may still have our fears, but we refuse to let them stand in our way of full recovery.

'No matter what' means our recovery is number one priority. We become disciplined in our approach to meditation or relaxation and in developing our cognitive skills. As our power and confidence develop, 'no matter what' means we challenge our thoughts. We challenge our fear. We challenge the anxiety and our attacks. How dare they do this to us?

The disorders do feel as if they push us to our limits, physically, mentally, emotionally and, in some cases, spiritually. We survive —but we can do more than just survive, we can recover. We can take back the power.

CHAPTER 7

STEP 3
MEDITATION:
WHY?

As I have shown throughout the book, our recovery depends on learning to manage our anxiety and attacks ourselves. Understanding and accepting our disorder are the first two steps to taking back our power. Learning to manage the attacks and the anxiety are the third and fourth steps.

The next three chapters look at meditation and how it can help us to relax and develop the all-important cognitive skill of mindfulness. We have been discussing dissociation and altered states of consciousness so it may seem unusual that I advocate the use of meditation. But meditation does work. This is how I recovered.

Meditation gave me the understanding I needed to learn to manage my attacks, anxiety and thoughts—to manage them to the point where I no longer need to manage them! I may dissociate if I am over-tired or feeling quite stressed, and I may have a full attack with the accompanying electric shock or burning heat. Even if I do, I no longer fear it and I am not at all anxious about it. My attitude towards it now is 'So what?'

Since my recovery I have been teaching meditation in my panic anxiety workshops (Hafner et al. 1996). I use meditation in a number of different ways—as a relaxation technique and as an exposure method to dissociative states, including depersonalisation and derealisation. Most people who do dissociate find meditation quite easy, because they are already accessing other states of consciousness through dissociation. We can use meditation as an exposure technique to become more familiar with altered states. The more familiar we become with them, the more we will lose our fear of them.

I also use meditation as a cognitive technique. This includes teaching people mindfulness, awareness skills and how not to attach to, or empower, the thoughts that turn on the fight-and-flight response. I also use meditation as an exposure method for letting go of the need to be in control and to stop fighting our panic attacks and anxiety. Meditation enables us to work with our disorder at our own pace and the more we practise, the more our overall cognitive and management techniques develop.

Meditation has been the subject of research since the late 1960s and is now being used in many treatments in conjunction with conventional medicine. Meditation also reduces anxiety levels in anxiety disorders. One study showed 'significant reductions in anxiety and depression' and demonstrated its effectiveness in panic disorder, with or without agoraphobia, and generalised anxiety disorder (Kabat-Zinn et al. 1992).

Learning to manage our anxiety and attacks means following a disciplined approach to a formal relaxation program. At first glance, some people hesitate. Although they want to recover they don't like the idea of having to be disciplined in their approach to it. Meditation is a superior relaxation technique if it is practised daily. In one way, 'having to relax' is a contradiction to the practice itself, but many of us find we reach the stage where we meditate because we want to, not because we have to.

Our recovery depends on our ability to bring down and keep down our anxiety level. Recovery means needing to change some of our previous ways of dealing with certain aspects of our life. Becoming disciplined in a relaxation technique is an important step in our overall commitment to recovery.

Background to meditation

Meditation is an integral part of Eastern religions and forms the basis of some Christian traditions. This gives rise to the many myths surrounding meditation. As a consequence some people are unsure of meditation and are concerned about practising it. If we have doubts about meditation because of our religious background, we need to speak to our minister or pastor and be guided by our own feelings of what is right for us.

Meditation is like many of the other Eastern techniques and disciplines we have adopted, such as the various martial arts, tai chi, qi gong and yoga. In India the word 'yoga' is a generic name for a multitude of meditation disciplines. Yoga was originally defined as 'the way to go'. For many of us who have recovered, it certainly was the way to go!

We associate yoga with the practice of gentle physical and breathing exercises. This form of yoga is derived from a very strict meditation discipline called hatha yoga. The West has adapted hatha yoga to its needs by stripping it of all its religious and ascetic practices. This form of yoga is now an accepted part of our Western lifestyle.

Other forms of meditation from Eastern traditions have also been adapted. The comprehensive and intricate visualisations of various deities have been replaced with images of beaches or forests, the devotional 'gazing' has been replaced with flowers or candles, and sacred mantras have been replaced with everyday words.

There is nothing mysterious in these techniques. The strict adherence and disciplines required for their religious and philosophical aspects have been stripped away, leaving their bare essence, which we use as techniques for relaxation. Learning to meditate does not mean we have to change our religion, our lifestyle or our diet. The only thing that will change will be our response to our attacks and our anxiety.

Misconceptions

We have other misconceptions about meditation. Some people see meditation as an escape from reality, or a selfish preoccupation. It is neither. A normal meditation time is twenty minutes twice a day. This hardly constitutes an escape from reality, nor can it be regarded as selfish. Everyone needs time to themselves. It is not selfish to want time alone, it is natural and normal.

Our disorder and any ensuing agoraphobia means we may not be able to contribute to our daily family situation as we did in the past. Practising meditation can mean a major step towards overall recovery. Recovery means we can contribute more, not only to the family but also to ourselves. Wanting to take time out, to help in the recovery process, is not selfish. It is looking after our self and our mental health.

Taking the time to stop and meditate can be a problem for some people. Meditation is usually practised for two twenty-minute periods each day, although a number of people meditate for only one twenty-minute period and still find it beneficial. Others tell themselves they can spare no time for meditation at all, despite the fact that their disorder may consume them twenty-four hours a day. It is a matter of making a choice regarding our priorities. It can mean the difference between ongoing anxiety and recovery.

Another myth about meditation is the idea that, when meditating, we may be leaving ourselves exposed to other influences. This does not and cannot happen. Even in the deepest phase of meditation we are always in complete control. We are always aware of everything within and outside ourselves. When we are asleep we are not consciously aware of anything, yet we will wake up should there be any internal or external threat. In meditation we don't need to 'become' aware because we are consciously aware, and consciously in control, the whole time.

The relaxation response

In his book The Relaxation Response (1975), Dr Herbert Benson discusses the meditative state that he calls the relaxation response and makes a comparison between the relaxation response and the fight-and-flight response, suggesting they are complete opposites. Both responses are controlled by an area of the brain called the hypothalamus. As the fight-and-flight response is a natural response that happens automatically in time of danger, Dr Benson suggests that the relaxation response—the meditative response—is also a natural response. As the fight-and-flight response causes much of our ongoing distress, the relaxation response, being its direct opposite, can help to ease it.

Learning to let go

In meditation, as in any relaxation technique, the first requirement is to let the relaxation process happen. It means not only letting go of our thoughts, feelings and emotions, but letting go of our control. As I mentioned in Chapter 3, our need to be in control of ourselves and our environment is one of the major factors in the perpetuation of the disorder. Letting go of this control is essential to recovery.

It may take some time for people to gain the confidence to begin to let go, but if we look at this closely we realise we let go every night when we go to sleep. Even if we have sleeping difficulties, we do eventually sleep. Letting go in meditation is the same as letting go and falling asleep.

When people experience difficulties in learning to relax, I advise them to sit and begin to meditate. If they feel afraid of letting go, they can either finish the meditation or allow the feelings of fear be there without getting caught up in them, while concentrating on their meditation technique. I advise those who decide to stop their meditation to practise again the next day and see if they are able to let go a little further. Sometimes, practising in small steps can ultimately give them the confidence to let go completely.

Other people are able to let go within meditation immediately, and as they let go they can meditate easily. This is the beginning of full recovery. It is a very important step because meditation teaches us that it is all right to let go of the control we are trying so hard to maintain. As we let go of this control we realise our major fears don't come true, and as our practice continues over time we begin to understand why they never will.

Some of us find the prospect of letting go in meditation quite fearful. It can be too frightening even to think about it. We may think that by letting go we will lose control, and all our worst fears will come true. This is not the case. By letting go we are actually gaining control, not losing it.

Sometimes we may experience an attack during meditation. This is how I actually learned to gain control over my attacks and anxiety. On occasions I would experience an attack during my meditation. I learned to let it happen in the same way as I had let go of the need to be in control. Instead of focusing on my thoughts of 'Oh, no, not again', I brought my attention back to my meditation technique. Much to my surprise the attacks disappeared as fast as they came and I realised I had discovered the key to my recovery.

Although this concept may seem frightening as you read this, in actuality it isn't. When you let the attack happen and keep focused on your meditation, the attack will move through your body and disappear as quickly as it came. This is taking back the power!

Learning about ourselves

Another beneficial aspect of meditation is that it can teach us about ourselves. Over a period of time and with continued practice, meditation begins to work on many subtle levels. The quiet of meditation gives us the chance to integrate many aspects of ourselves. This happens subconsciously and we don't become aware of this process straight away. Slowly and subtly the integration breaks through into our consciousness. We begin to see changes in how we perceive and react to day-to-day situations.

A useful analogy to describe this is when we use the 'sort' command on a database to arrange it in alphabetical or numerical order. We press the 'sort' key and the computer rearranges the information into the order we need.

Meditation works something like this. It helps to process all the information we are holding in our 'database'. It begins to sort everything into a more ordered view. Sometimes the process of meditation will 'throw out a file' for us to look at, other times it gets on with what it has to do without any reference to us. The end result is a changed and clearer perception of ourselves and our environment.

This is part of the reason why meditation and psychotherapy 'complement' one another. One study of meditation states that 'meditation may facilitate the psychotherapeutic process' (Task Force on Meditation 1977). Meditation can assist us in 'sorting through' the various issues and difficulties we have had in our life. If we combine this sorting through process with the sorting through process of psychotherapy, we may be able to access insights and solutions more easily.

The release of stress

Each meditation session needs to last for twenty minutes. In the case of meditation, more is not necessarily better. Within the twenty minutes, accumulated stress and emotions can be released. This is 'sorting through'. It is better if this release is done slowly and gradually. If our meditation time is extended, it is possible that feelings such as grief, sadness or anger, of which we were unaware, will arise. As I said, it will sometimes 'throw out a file' for us to look at.

On rare occasions this may happen during the twenty-minute session. This frightens people sometimes, but this releasing process is very necessary for our overall mental health! If it does happen and we feel distressed, we can reduce the meditation time to ten minutes, gradually building back up to twenty minutes. It is better to cut down the length of our meditation rather than stop meditating altogether.

After twelve or eighteen months of regular meditation, session times can be slowly extended up to an hour. The releasing process is an ongoing one but, with experience, people are able to understand and not become hesitant if they experience a release of feelings or emotions. Many people actually cultivate such releases because they see how beneficial they are in the long term.

Guide to successful meditation

While the meditation process produces a feeling of quiet, don't expect it to happen. Just let the meditation process happen naturally and easily. If we expect it to happen, it doesn't. If we expect it to happen, we spend the whole meditation session not meditating but looking for the quiet and wondering when it will happen. When we are meditating correctly our meditation will lead us effortlessly and naturally to the full meditative state. Don't fight thoughts, feelings or emotions. Let them come and let them go. Don't become involved with them by hooking into them. Meditation is not a process of trying to eliminate all thoughts or feelings. Nor is it a process of trying to think of nothing, which is a contradiction in itself. The 'no-thinking' will happen naturally as we move into the deeper stages. The rising and falling of our thoughts are part of the whole process. They will slow down and finally cease naturally as we enter the full meditative state.

- As the meditation process unfolds, some people become anxious when they notice their breathing slowing down. Sometimes it feels as if they are hardly breathing at all. This can be disconcerting at first, especially for people who have this fear. There is nothing to worry about. The slowing down of our breathing indicates we are beginning to relax deeply. It is a definitive sign that the meditation session is going well.
- When using a word or mantra to meditate, don't worry when it becomes distorted or disappears altogether in the course of meditation. This is another indication of successful meditation.
- Some people find they go to sleep during meditation. Although meditation teachers advise their students to remain alert and not go to sleep, I feel somewhat differently about it in the case of anxiety disorders. We are already under enough pressure from our disorder. Setting rules about what we can and can't do in the practice of meditation only gives us more things to worry about, not to mention trying to meditate perfectly every time. If we can let go and relax enough to sleep, then initially this is all that matters.

  Many people who have an anxiety disorder have difficulty sleeping. If meditation means people are able to catch up on sleep, then the practice is successful. Most people who do go to sleep during meditation find they do so for about forty-five minutes, and on awakening they feel the benefits. Take it as it comes. In time we all reach the stage when we actually meditate instead of going to sleep.
- Don't set an alarm clock to time the meditation session. There is nothing worse than being brought out of meditation by a

loud noise. It is quite easy to time a meditation. Most of us place a watch in a convenient position and during the meditation will open our eyes to check the time. After a few days most of us are able to gauge when the twenty minutes are over without needing to check.

Sometimes the twenty minutes pass so quickly we wonder if our watches are working correctly; on other occasions the time seems to go very slowly and we become irritated. If this happens, it may be beneficial to end the meditation session and try again later.

When the meditation session is over, we need to sit quietly with our eyes closed for a couple of minutes before getting up. This allows us to reorient ourselves gently and naturally. There may be times when we need to break our meditation session for one reason or another. If this happens, try to return to it as soon as possible to finish the remaining time.

- Outside noises may interfere. Acknowledge they are there but don't become caught up in them. Let them happen and let go of the irritated thoughts.

- Avoid drinking coffee and other products that use caffeine before meditation. Caffeine is a stimulant. Meditation is for relaxation. It is also a good idea not to meditate just after eating, because the digestive system slows down during meditation.

- Initially, each meditation session will be different from the previous one. Some will be great, others not so good. Remember that learning to meditate is learning a new skill. For the first twelve months most people find each of their meditation sessions is different. It is this difference that teaches us more about the whole process.

- It is important to go with whatever happens. Don't stifle a cough or a yawn or a sneeze. Do whatever feels and is comfortable.

- The daily practice of meditation does require discipline, but we shouldn't feel guilty if we miss a meditation session. Missing one or two sessions happens to everyone. Only after days turn into a week or more without practice should we seriously question our motivation—or lack of it.

CHAPTER 8

STEP 3 MEDITATION: HOW?

The word technique

The first meditation technique I discuss is derived from a yoga discipline called *mantra yoga*. While hatha yoga uses breathing and physical exercise to enter the meditative state, mantra yoga uses a mantra—a sound or a devotional word or phrase that we silently repeat to ourselves. 'Om', which is pronounced 'aum', is a mantra most of us have heard of.

The Western adaptation of mantra yoga uses a word instead of the traditional mantra. This meditation technique involves the silent repetition of a word to focus our minds on. This technique is not used in conjunction with a breathing technique. All it involves is the repetition of a word.

CHOOSING A WORD

What word to use is a matter of individual choice. As a general guide, make sure the word is short. Some people use the word 'hush' or 'quiet'. Depending on a person's religious background, they may choose a word that has a deeper meaning for them. Dr Herbert Benson (1975) in *The Relaxation Response* uses the word 'one'.

I have found it better to stay away from words such as 'peace' or 'calm'. We have so many negative associations with these words— 'Calm down', 'Why can't I get any peace?'—that we may have difficulty meditating.

CHOOSING A MANTRA

Some people choose to use a mantra. The familiar mantra 'aum' has been translated as meaning 'the sound of the universe'. Two other well known mantras are 'sharma', which has been translated as 'quietude', and 'shantih', meaning 'peace' or 'calm'.

The word or mantra is used as a focal point during the meditation. As our practice continues we become conditioned to our word or mantra, and over time it becomes associated with the deeper levels of meditation. This makes our practice of meditation easier, because the word or mantra will take us directly to the deeper levels of meditation without us having to go through the preliminary stages. This is why it is preferable not to continually change your word or mantra. Changing it can lead to frustration with the whole process. We need to become relaxed, not frustrated.

The only exception to this is when a word, mantra or even an image comes spontaneously into our mind during a meditation session. If this happens then use that word, mantra or image. Meditation teaches us in sometimes very subtle ways. It helps us to reconnect back to our self. The spontaneous rising of a word, mantra or image is part this.

CONFUSION

People occasionally become confused over their choice of word. They spend many meditation sessions experimenting with one word or another, and consequently do not achieve any results whatsoever. In such cases it is a good idea to use a breathing technique instead.

Breathing techniques

The breathing techniques I will discuss are based on the Buddhist mindfulness meditation, which focuses on the breath. This can be frightening for people who have fears associated with their breathing. While this technique does not involve deep breathing, it may be more advisable for these people to use the word technique instead.

There are two ways of using the breathing technique. In both cases, it does not mean we need to take deep breaths, or slow our breathing down. We simply breathe normally. The first technique is being 'mindful' of our breathing—watching the breathing process, watching the rise and fall of our breath, as we inhale and exhale. The act of watching the breath becomes the focus. Simple!

The second way is to count each breath. Counting each breath becomes the technique. As we begin to meditate, the first breath we take is counted as 'one', the second 'two' and so on until breath number five. After breath number five the count begins again at 'one', and so on.

Sometimes people use both a word and the first breathing technique. This will not cause any problems and, if it feels right, then use them both. At this stage, however, it is better to decide on one technique and then stay with it.

Many people find that playing a piece of meditation or classical music in the background is quite beneficial as it helps to block out distracting sounds. It also helps them to let go more easily.

It is best not to use the word, mantra or breathing technique during our normal daily life when we are anxious or having an attack. As our technique becomes linked to the meditative state, the last thing we need is to find we have begun to associate it with anxiety and attacks.

The practice of meditation

Sit comfortably in a chair and close your eyes. After a few seconds, begin to concentrate lightly on either the silent repetition of the word or the breathing technique. There is no need for intense concentration. Just be aware as you silently repeat your word or focus on your breathing. Thoughts will intrude. This is normal. Our thoughts are a part of the process of meditation. In the early stages it is very easy to get caught up in the thoughts. We need to become aware, we need to be mindful, that we are thinking, not meditating. Gently let the thoughts go, stop concentrating on them or thinking about them and return your awareness to the word or the breath. Thoughts will break through again and again! Be aware, let them go and come back to the word or the breath.

It is important not to worry about the thoughts that break through. This is the one basic mistake most of us make in meditation. When we first learn to meditate we constantly get caught up in our thoughts. We need to learn to be mindful, be aware, let them go and return to the word or the breath. As our skill develops, our minds become more disciplined and settle much more easily.

The process of meditation can be summarised as follows:

1. As we begin the practice of meditation we bring our attention either to silently repeating a word or mantra, or focusing on our breathing.
2. Our thoughts break through and we get caught up in our thinking.

3. We become mindful we are thinking, not meditating.
4. We let go of our thoughts and we . . .
1. Return to the word or the breath.
2. Again we become caught up in our thoughts.
3. We again become mindful we are thinking.
4. We let go of our thoughts and we . . .
1. Return to the word or the breath.

This is the process of meditation. These are the four stages everyone works through. This is also the first stage of learning to develop control over our thoughts. It is no wonder that Eastern traditions refer to 'the monkey mind'. As we learn to meditate we begin to see how much our thoughts run and jump all over the place!

There are two ways people experience the preliminary stages of meditation. Some people will be able to focus their attention on their chosen technique, and that is all they need to do to free their minds from any other thought. Their attention will be broken as a thought rises into consciousness. The thought then becomes the focus of attention and their technique will disappear completely. When they become mindful and bring their attention back to the word or breath their thoughts will disappear.

Other people will be aware of the repetition of their word or aware of their breath, plus the rise and fall of thoughts at the same time. The rise and fall of their thoughts may be in the 'background' while their attention is focused on their technique in the 'foreground', or vice versa. When they become aware their attention is on their thoughts, they let them go and the thoughts drift into the background again.

CASE HISTORIES

Philip

Deciding to find time to meditate can be a problem for many people, of whom Philip was one. Philip had been practising meditation on and off for several months. He had become aware that he always had a bad day if he didn't meditate the night before, but wished there was an easier way to control his anxiety. He 'didn't have time' and it was such an effort to try to make time to meditate. He felt he would just have to put up with the anxiety until a 'real' cure was found.

Joanne

'I did it, I did it,' Joanne told her husband. 'I was so scared when we started. Then I did feel myself relaxing, and that scared me. It has been so long since I have relaxed, I got confused and that made me anxious. But I just let it happen and kept my mind focused on the word and then I realised it was just the tension draining away. And I felt great. Then I had an attack. I couldn't believe it. I was so relaxed. But I kept on going. I let that happen as well. And it disappeared so fast. It just shot through me and it was gone. I just kept focusing on my word and I just went deeper and deeper into meditation. Then suddenly the time was up. I didn't want it to end. I felt so fantastic.'

Stages of meditation

There are several stages in the meditative process. Most people experience them in varying degrees, although it does not matter if people never experience them. Some people do become worried about these experiences so it is important to discuss them.

The one experience people worry about is the sensation of their body relaxing. Sometimes people have been so tense for so many years they have forgotten what it is like to feel even slightly relaxed. As their bodies begin to let go of the tension, people become anxious and interpret these sensations as a sign that their worst fears are about to come true. They don't. It is simply the body relaxing!

The first stage of meditation can be difficult for beginners. Our thoughts are not used to being ignored and they continually break through and demand attention. As long as we can accept this as normal and let go of them without becoming frustrated, we can move into the second stage of meditation.

As we enter the second stage of meditation we feel the quiet settle over us. Whether we are focusing on a word or on our breathing we all find our breathing begins to slow down. Our thoughts are still rising and falling but our attention is now much more focused on the word or breath. All external sound moves into the background with our thoughts as our quietness grows.

We enter the third stage. Our breathing slows down even further and our body becomes deeply relaxed. We may feel as if we are as light as a feather, or we may feel a comfortable heaviness. We become aware that the continuous stream of thoughts has broken. They now rise slowly and separate from each other. Individually, they quietly rise and fall without us becoming distracted by them. We find our word or mantra becomes distorted. This is what is supposed to happen. Some of us may see brilliant white, black or other swirls of colour. We can use them to take ourselves deeper. Our thoughts drift in and out, slowly and quietly.

We then enter the full meditative state in which there is perfect quietness, an absence of thought, feeling or emotions. Unlike the stages of deep sleep, this state of consciousness is very dynamic. There is full awareness of 'nothing', but in that 'no-thing' is an awareness of 'every-thing'. In this state there is no technique and no thoughts or feelings—just an all-pervasive quiet. Yet we are aware of everything and in full control. When we think 'This is wonderful', the quiet is broken by the thought, but we can return to the quiet simply by returning to the word or the breath.

This is meditation.

CHAPTER 9

STEP 4
DEVELOPING
MINDFULNESS

'What if?' How many times during the course of the disorder have we all said this in one form or another—'What if I have an attack?' 'What if something happens?' 'What if I make a fool of myself?' How many times has the anxiety and panic stopped us from doing what we wanted to do? How many times have we spent days, weeks or months worrying about 'what if'? What if this is perpetuating our disorder? It is.

Thinking about it

Irrespective of our disorder, recovery is the loss of fear of our attacks and the loss of fear of all the many and varied fears we all have. We give our thoughts the power and our thoughts destroy our lives. Everyone tells us: 'It is mind over matter' or 'You should just stop thinking about it' or 'You are always thinking about it'. And this is exactly what we need to do. We need to stop thinking about it. We need to get to the point where it is mind over matter—we don't really mind because it doesn't really matter. In other words, we don't mind if we do have an attack because it *really doesn't matter!* 'So what!'

It is difficult for most people who haven't experienced a panic attack and/or our levels of anxiety to understand why we can't stop thinking about it and why we can't 'pull ourselves together'. If it were that simple we wouldn't have the disorder. It is no use trying to 'think positive', because many of us do not believe the positive statements we say to ourselves. Even though we are told repeatedly that nothing is going to happen to us, it is difficult to believe when we are constantly betrayed by the attacks and anxiety. We think the next attack is going to be 'the big one' in which our fears will be realised. We can't just 'not think about it' when we live and breathe it every day. This is the problem, we live and breathe it, because we constantly think about it!

Our thinking is so much a part of us we don't pay any attention to the process. Without realising it, our thoughts create, dictate and control our life. We all know the endless silent conversations, the chattering thoughts and the continual negative cycles of thinking. They roll along, carrying us with them. Yet it need not be like this. We can step in and take back the power by learning to control them. Our lives do not have to be dictated by them. We can dictate to them.

The 'what ifs' are part of the control we all use. They are part of our overall defence strategy which needs to have every possible scenario covered, just in case! The 'what ifs' and the continual monitoring of our symptoms don't protect us or provide us with an 'early warning system' because they create the very symptoms we are trying to protect ourselves from.

We create the fear by the way we think. We never take time to examine our thoughts. We don't even realise we can. We never watch our thoughts as they spin this way and that. We react to our thoughts without realising they are actually separate fleeting moments in time. Instead, we believe we have no power over the continual progression of our thoughts, and the feelings caused by them. We don't see how our feelings can change within seconds of a change in our thought pattern. We can be feeling happy one minute and anxious the next. Not seeing this progression from one thought to another and not seeing the progression from one feeling to another, makes it appear that our anxiety and attacks are beyond our control. They aren't.

Changing our perception

Taking back the power means changing the way we perceive the attacks and the anxiety. We see them as being life-threatening, or a threat to our sanity, or as ultimately causing us to lose control. There is no doubt the anxiety can cause extreme discomfort and the attacks can feel quite violent, but they are not life-threatening nor a sign of impending insanity nor a sign we are going to lose control in some way. We compound our disorder by continually thinking of 'worst case scenarios'. We need to see the anxiety and the attacks for what they really are: anxiety and attacks. Nothing more. This is the perception change. When we can see and *believe* this, our anxiety over our anxiety and panic diminishes and our attacks disappear as quickly as they come.

Recovery for many of us means that, occasionally, we may still have an attack but, because we do not fear it, it flashes through and is over in a matter of thirty seconds or so. Not hours or days which turn into weeks or years as a result of our anxiety and fears. As we do not fear it, the fight-and-flight response is not turned on, so we do not become caught up in the panic and anxiety cycle.

Everyone says, 'I don't want to have one even for thirty seconds, I never want to have another one.' Fair enough! When we are caught up in our disorder this is a natural response. But the reality is that we may still have an attack when we are over-tired or stressed, particularly if we have the ability to dissociate. We are more vulnerable to dissociation when we are over-tired, skipping meals or eating on the run.

As we recover, we develop a far deeper understanding of our attacks, anxiety and panic and it is this deeper understanding that empowers us to be able to say 'So what!' When we are caught up in the panic and anxiety cycle we do not have the understanding to enable us to do this.

It is difficult for many people to believe recovery is possible. After trying many different methods without success, it is difficult to believe anything will succeed. If we think something isn't going to work, then it won't. That's our problem—our thinking.

We need to be in control of ourselves and our environment, yet the only thing we do not control is our thinking. We need to change this by letting go of the overall need to be in control, and control our thinking instead.

CASE HISTORIES

Jan

The wedding of Jan's daughter was six months away and the planning for it was gaining momentum. Instead of feeling excited, Jan was feeling desperate. What if she had a panic attack on the day of the wedding? What if she had to leave the church or the reception? What would everyone think? She didn't want to make a fool of herself or disrupt the wedding in any way. What if she couldn't make it to the wedding at all? She was feeling anxious about it already, yet it was still six months away. Jan wanted to prevent her anxiety from increasing, but she didn't know how.

Marilyn

Marilyn's counsellor had told her that clinging to the memory of her first panic attack was not helping her as she worked on her recovery. Marilyn felt quite angry with the counsellor. What did the counsellor know anyway? That first panic attack was dreadful. Marilyn had been in the local shopping mall when it happened. She had no idea what it was and had thought she was dying. She had asked a few people to help her but they didn't respond. They must have thought she was either drunk or crazy. Marilyn had had to get back to her car by herself and drive herself home, where she stayed for the next four years. Although she had made it home safely every time she had tried to go out since then, Marilyn would think of her first attack and naturally she would become anxious. She didn't want to go through that again. How could she not think about that attack? It was that attack that caused all the ongoing problems. Marilyn thought the counsellor, like all the rest she had seen, didn't really understand and wouldn't be able to help her.

Learning to change our perception

Working with our thinking is a three-stage process, but before we can begin to do this we need to bring our self back to this moment in time. All of us are basing this moment in time on the suffering we have experienced in the past. Not only that, we are basing our future on our past suffering.

Our lack of understanding about our disorder has, in many cases, meant years of suffering and to many people it seems that the future will be no different. But it can be. The past belongs to the past—except for one major point. Despite the enormous difficulties we have encountered through the disorder, nothing has physically happened to us. Our lives may have been destroyed by our disorder, but none of our major fears has been realised, and they aren't going to be in the future. It is the way we are thinking and perceiving our attacks and anxiety that does the damage. It is our perception that has created the turmoil in our lives. The next attack is not going to be the 'big one' in which our fears come true. If anything were going to happen to us it would have happened in the first attack.

We continually draw on our fears of our past experiences of the anxiety and attacks and we project them into the future—which, incidentally, is only a moment away. We don't concentrate on what is happening now in this moment in time.

As an example, what are our first thoughts when we wake in the morning? The first thought is usually 'Where is it?' and we feel frightened because we know 'it' is going to be there. We turn on our internal radar and check to see what is happening. We move down our body. 'I'm going to have a headache, my throat is tight, my heart is racing, I'm having trouble breathing, I feel sick, I'm shaking.' And our anxiety soars. As we go to sleep at night we think to ourselves, 'What if I am still anxious or have an attack in the morning?'

If we always have an attack at 7 a.m. we expect to have one every morning. When we have an attack we think 'I knew it would happen'. We expect to have one the following morning, and we do. We don't see what is happening now because we are too busy anticipating and thinking about the next attack.

We need to let go of the past, except for two important points. First, nothing is going to happen to us as a result of our panic and anxiety. We are living, breathing, sane proof of this. We now need to start believing it. Second, as we move through the recovery process we will begin to grieve for everything we have lost as a result of our disorder. And we will grieve for the biggest loss of all, the loss of our self, the person we thought we were before we developed the disorder. This grieving process is natural, normal and healthy.

We need to let go of everything else. We need to let go of our perceptions and fears and what we think will happen, may happen, should happen, shouldn't happen, could happen, couldn't happen as a result of our anxiety and panic.

As I said in the opening chapter, everyone always says, if they had known, understood and learnt to manage their attacks and their anxiety from the beginning, then they would never have developed the disorder in the first place. And this is what we need to do right now. We need to begin again in this moment of time.

We experience panic and anxiety, and now many of us know intellectually that our experience is panic and anxiety. We may also know intellectually that our fears will not come true. But, and it is a big 'but'—emotionally we don't. This is the critical point and it is why so many of us struggle despite our intellectual understanding of our experience. Emotionally we do not believe it.

We get caught up in our fears about our attacks and anxiety and we sabotage our intellectual understanding of our disorder on a daily basis. We need to bring our emotional understanding of our disorder to the same understanding we have of it intellectually. When I talk of a change of perception, this is what I mean. Emotionally, we learn to perceive our experience as it is, for what it is—panic and anxiety, nothing more. This is why those of us who have recovered can now say 'So what!' because we believe it intellectually and emotionally.

The process of recovery is learning to understand and believe emotionally why our various fears will not come true; learning to understand emotionally how our experience is being created, moment to moment, thought by thought.

Taking back the power: mindfulness

The first step is to become mindful of what is actually happening in the moment. We know we are thinking negatively but, emotionally, we are not really aware of how this creates so much of our distress. Emotionally, we need to get 'behind the scenes' of our negative thinking and see, step by step, how our thoughts create so much of our experience.

To do this we draw on the cognitive principles inherent in the practice of meditation, but in this instance we will not be meditating. We will use these cognitive elements to show us the overall operating dynamics of our experience, the cause and the effect.

Initially, this cognitive technique may appear to be an intellectual exercise going nowhere. It isn't. Rather, it is retraining our emotional understanding so that it integrates with our intellectual understanding of disorder. This is key to recovery.

Part of meditation is being aware, being mindful of when we get caught up in our thoughts. We use the basic principle of being aware, of being mindful, of what we are thinking about in daily life. Part of us needs to stand back and watch the whole process. In the beginning all we need to do is to observe our thoughts. To become mindful of what we are thinking about. Don't analyse them or interfere with them. Just watch them as they come tumbling in. We need to become mindful of the contents of our thoughts.

We may not be thinking about our anxiety or panic, but whatever we are thinking about is going to be negative. Be aware of the negative conversations we have in our head. We reenact scenarios about things in our life that have happened, could happen, should happen, shouldn't have happened, in a hundred different ways. We need to become aware of how we hook into the guilt thoughts, the mental self-abuse thoughts—'I'm stupid, hopeless, dumb'—how we hook into thoughts of hopelessness and helplessness.

Some people need to be mindful of the thought: 'I don't want to know about this. It is too frightening!' If we are frightened to look at the content of our thoughts, then we are not going to recover because all we are doing is being frightened of the actual cause of our distress. All this does is add another component to our fears.

As we become more mindful of the content of our thoughts we then need to bring this awareness to our bodies. Our thoughts are the cause, our symptoms are the effect. We need to be aware of how our body is responding to our thoughts, how our fears and anxiety are being created moment to moment. It isn't the symptoms that create our thoughts. It is our thoughts that create the fear, which turns on the fight-and-flight response, which in turn creates our symptoms, which creates more thoughts, more fear, and round and round we go. We need to become mindful of the whole process.

If I ask people what they were thinking about before their last attack, they usually say they weren't thinking of anything. This is not so. They were thinking, they just weren't aware of their thoughts. Asking the same question of people who feel continually anxious brings the same reply. They also are not aware.

We need to be aware of the relationship between our thoughts, our fears and our symptoms. When we can actually see this relationship and the overall operating dynamics of it, we begin to understand it emotionally. We begin to understand emotionally how our fears are being created, sometimes moment to moment. We begin to understand emotionally why there is actually nothing to fear—that our anxiety and the panic are the effects of our thinking. We are simply frightening ourselves, nothing more. This is the change of perception. The more we practise, the more our perception of our experience changes and, ultimately, our emotional understanding integrates with that of our intellectual understanding and we are free!

We also begin to see how almost all our thoughts have the potential to create our anxiety and panic. As I said above, whatever we are thinking about, it is negative. These thoughts also place us in 'danger' and the fight-and-flight response is activated. Our guilt thoughts, our internal critic, our thoughts of hopelessness, helplessness, worthlessness are threatening to us because they deny and invalidate the integrity of self, of who we actually are. I discuss this in the next chapter.

DISSOCIATION

Becoming aware and being mindful also applies to people who dissociate first and become frightened and panic as a result. We need to become mindful of how we are actually inducing a trance state. We need to be mindful if we are staring, or locked into a self-absorbed state; we need to be mindful when we are around fluorescent lighting.

This doesn't mean we add more fears to our catalogue of fears. 'What if I stare? There is fluorescent lighting in the supermarket. I can't go there in case I have an attack.' It is a matter of being mindful of the triggers, so that if we do trance out we will know the reasons why. The more familiar we can become with our ability to dissociate the less fear we will have of it and the easier it will be to manage. We can simply break our stare or the effects of the fluorescent lights by blinking and moving our head, or by bringing ourselves out of an absorbed state.

When we are afraid of our ability to dissociate, we need to become mindful of our thoughts. 'What's happening to me? Here it comes again. I'm going insane.' We need to become mindful of how our thoughts create the fear that creates the anxiety and panic.

We can stop the escalation into anxiety and panic simply by being mindful. 'I'm dissociating. I've just gone into a trance state.' When we acknowledge what is happening to us, without letting our thoughts race out of control, we can break the dissociated state very easily by breaking our stare or blinking our eyes a few times. When our thoughts race away with how terrible it all is, our fear will not only hold us in the altered state but will create even more symptoms.

Taking back the power: letting go

As we become mindful of our thoughts and their impact on us, we begin to see we have a choice. If we keep on thinking in the way we do, we know where it is going to take us—straight to anxiety and panic. The second step is learning to control our thoughts instead of them controlling us. This is not the avoidance of thoughts by trying to distract ourselves in some way—that only creates further anxiety.

Again we draw on the cognitive elements of meditation. In meditation we become mindful that we are thinking and not meditating and we let go of our thoughts and return to the word or breath. This time we will draw on the 'letting-go' process of meditation but we will not be using our word or breath as a focus as we normally do in 'formal' meditation sessions. In normal waking hours this would become more of a distraction technique. And distraction techniques do not, nor will they ever, give us long-term recovery. Distraction can become an avoidance technique. If we try to avoid our thoughts, all we are doing is giving them even more power over us.

The secret of controlling our thinking is being able to let our thoughts go, not to become involved with them. It is not a matter of fighting the thoughts or trying to stop them or avoid them. It is simply letting them come into consciousness and then letting them go, as we do in meditation. In the beginning it is very important that we acknowledge our thoughts. This helps us to ensure that we are not avoiding them or trying to distract ourselves from them. It also assists us in understanding our thought patterns even more.

When we are being mindful, we see our thoughts and we see the choice we have of whether to get hooked up in them. We can consciously choose not to get involved with them. Before we let them go, we acknowledge them by naming them 'anxiety' thought, 'panic' thought, 'depressive' thought, 'internal critic' thought, 'negative' thought, 'guilt' thought, and so on. We acknowledge them and then we let them go. This means that we don't think on them, we don't hook into them, we simply stop them by letting them go. In one way we become our own 'thought police'. We take control and begin to direct the thought 'traffic'. This is the hard part. As soon as we let go of one thought another is there to take its place. We let go of that and another comes. But we learn to become involved in the letting-go cycle, not the panic and anxiety cycle.

This is where we need a lot of discipline. Remember, we are learning a new skill and it is going to take time and patience. In essence, what we are doing is learning to gain control over our thoughts and, in doing so, taking back the power from the disorder. With practice, we become caught up in the letting-go process instead of becoming caught up in our thoughts.

Taking back the power: What if? So what!

When we are first learning to take back the power from our thoughts we will still have anxiety symptoms and in all probability we will still experience attacks. Our normal reaction to the anxiety and the attacks is to fight them and try to stop them from happening. This only increases them. Notice the word *fight*. When we fight them, all we are doing is turning on the fight-and-flight response. The final step in taking back the power is to learn to feel whatever we are feeling by letting our attacks and anxiety symptoms happen without trying to resist them or control them.

Some people will say they would never have the courage to let an attack or the anxiety happen, and that it is only natural to fight against it. I agree it is natural to want to fight against it, but fighting it by resisting it only makes it worse.

We are all very strong people and we need to recognise this. It takes a significant amount of strength and courage to live with anxiety and panic on a daily basis. We already have the strength and the courage. It is a matter of choosing which way we want to use them. Whether we use our strength and courage to take back our power by learning to let our attacks and anxiety happen, or whether we use it to hold on to our pervasive need to be in control is a matter of choice. Choosing to use our strength and courage to let the attack and the anxiety happen will teach us why there is nothing to fear. When we can let them happen, they disappear because we are not adding to them by fighting them.

What did you think when you read that you need to let the attack and the symptoms of anxiety happen? Did you think 'I can't do that. What will happen? How can I let it happen?' How did you respond physically? Did you feel anxious? You probably did. Most people do when they first hear this. Did the anxiety or the negative thoughts come first? It was the thoughts that came first and the symptoms that followed.

To learn to let the symptoms happen means we draw on the meditation technique again. In meditation we let go of our thoughts and we let the meditation happen without trying to control it in any way. We can also learn to do this when we are experiencing anxiety or a full attack, including the burning, tingling heat or 'electric shock' feelings. We let them happen. We do not interfere with them, we don't fight them, we don't avoid them or try to distract ourselves from the feelings, we simply let them happen.

When we fight the attack it can last for over an hour. When we fight the anxiety it can last for days, weeks, even years. When we totally give in to it and let it happen an attack can disappear within thirty seconds because it is not being fuelled by the fight-and-flight response. The same applies to our anxiety, although our anxiety can stay if we continually monitor it and think to ourselves, 'I am letting it happen so why doesn't it go away?' It is a matter of learning to let the anxiety and the attack be there without getting caught up in them.

As an example, what happens when we feel happy? Do we check our body for the signs of happiness: 'My head is happy; my throat is happy; my heartbeat is happy; my breathing is happy; my stomach is happy' and so on? Of course we don't. We let the feelings of happiness be there and we don't hook into our thoughts of 'I'm happy, happy, happy!' We simply feel happy and get on with whatever we are doing.

So why can't we do this with the anxiety and the attack? If we are anxious, we can allow our self to feel anxious. We don't need to get involved with it. If we have an attack, we can let ourselves have an attack.

The more mindful we become, the more we see and understand, at an emotional level, why there is nothing to fear from our anxiety or attacks. The more we understand about the dynamics of our experience, the easier it is to let them happen without getting caught up in the cycle. When we can do this, we are finally able to take back the power. Fighting to control our anxiety and attacks perpetuates them. When we let them happen, we destroy them, because we are not adding to them through fear.

The first time we let an attack happen there may be an increase in the intensity of the attack. This happens because we are thinking 'What if something happens?' Go with this onrush of fear. Let this happen too. When we are able to give up the fight and give in to an attack without resisting it, it will disappear so fast it will scare us further. 'Where is it? Where did it go?' 'It' will only return if we don't let go of our fearful thinking.

Anger: the rocketship to recovery

The more mindful we become the more frustrated we will become. We let go of our thoughts and there are ten more queuing up for their chance to try to frighten us. Moving into the frustration stage means we are beginning to see and feel emotionally why there is nothing to fear. Becoming frustrated can be a pivotal point for us to become angry, really angry—not with our self, but with our attacks, the anxiety, and their effects on our life. Anger directed at our disorder is the rocket-ship to recovery. Why aren't we angry? Our disorder can destroy our life. Why aren't we angry at this? Why are we being so passive toward it? Why are we letting the disorder do this to us? How dare it do this to us!

Many people are frightened of feeling their anger and I discuss this in the next chapter, but anger in response to our disorder is healthy. When we can direct the full extent of our anger at the anxiety, the fears and the attacks, they disappear so quickly that it can frighten us because we wonder if they are regrouping for the 'big' one. They aren't! Anger can herald the final shift in our perception and our emotional beliefs. When we can use the full weight of our anger against the disorder, we take back our power.

What will people think?

Countless people have told me that they can't let an attack or the anxiety just happen because they are worried other people may see it happening. So what if they do? Why are we risking our mental health for the sake of everyone else? We can spend all day trying to hide our symptoms from employers, work colleagues, family and friends. The extraordinary energy and control we use to hide our symptoms only makes us more anxious and exhausted. The more anxious we become the more we have to hide it.

Taking back the power means we cannot let the fear of what other people think get in our way of full recovery. If our hands and legs shake, let them shake. If our face turns bright red, then our face turns bright red. If we are perspiring profusely, then we are perspiring profusely. If we feel faint, sit down on a chair, on the floor, on the footpath if need be. If we vomit or have an attack of diarrhoea, then we vomit or have an attack of diarrhoea. Let it happen. When we let it happen, we turn off the fight-and-flight response and it will be over as quickly as it starts. We will not have to waste all our energy trying to keep it under control.

Our mental health needs to be considered more important than other people's opinions. The feelings of embarrassment are created by our thoughts. We need to move from 'What if?' to the all-powerful attitude of 'So what?' So what if we have an attack? So what if we are feeling anxious? So what if people see? So what?

How high our anxiety level is will affect how quickly the anxiety disappears. Learning to manage the anxiety by being aware of our thoughts, letting them go and allowing the anxiety to be there is part of the recovery process. But as we become more mindful, we will see how much of our overall anxiety is created when we are not being true to ourselves, when we are giving 'ourselves' away because of our fear of what people will think.

With practice we will reach the point where we will have a choice in how we respond to our anxiety and attacks, either with fear or by letting them happen. This choice will always be there. After recovery we may experience further attacks in times of extreme stress. We can choose how we respond: either with fear—'What if?'—or by letting go and letting it happen. So what?

Have you ever *tried* to have an attack? Have you ever *tried* to be anxious? Try. See what happens.

CHAPTER 10

STEP 5
WORKING
THROUGH TO
RECOVERY

Many people do not give their recovery priority. Although everyone wants to recover, there seems to be a million more important things to be done first, usually for everyone else! Our recovery has to become the most important thing in our life. It needs to be our number one priority.

This can very difficult for many of us because we feel we are being selfish in putting our own needs first. But we need to ask ourselves: 'How can working towards our recovery be selfish?' In the working-through process, especially at the beginning, we need our energy for ourselves. Part of the recovery process means accepting that we don't need to go along with what other people expect from us. We don't have to do, or accept, anything we know is going to be detrimental to ourselves and/or our recovery. Our mental health depends on nothing less!

The working-through process

Recovery is not as simple as we would like it to be. In the beginning, it feels as though we take one step forward then two steps backwards. This is why so many people feel they are never going to recover. It is also part of the reason why so many people become discouraged and give up.

We need to understand the step-by-step process of working through the various stages of recovery. Understanding the working-through process is of the utmost importance, yet in treatment options it is still rarely given the importance it merits.

Patience

One of the first things we need to learn is patience. Everyone, naturally enough, wants recovery now. Not tonight, not tomorrow, not next week, but this very second. All this does is create further stress which keeps the whole cycle going. Whether we like it or not, we all need to learn patience with the working-through process and with ourselves. Learning to be patient is learning to be kind to ourselves. Being kind to ourselves means we are not putting ourselves under any further unnecessary stress.

We need to direct our energy into the determination to commit ourselves, time and again, to the working-through process despite setbacks. While the word 'setbacks' may appear to be negative, in reality it isn't. As we progress further down the path of recovery, setbacks actually become our teachers.

In Chapter 5 I spoke about needing to bring our emotional development up to the level of our intellectual development, and this is what setbacks do. They demonstrate very clearly when we are holding our emotional development back. They teach us when we are not being responsible for ourselves, when we are invalidating ourselves by trying to be who we think we should be.

In the early stages of recovery we don't see this constructive aspect of our setbacks. In the beginning we see them simply as setbacks that are frustrating, frightening and signs (we think) that we won't ever recover. We will, if we are totally committed and determined.

Our stress threshold

The working-through process may at first seem difficult and confusing and some people feel daunted and overwhelmed by the amount of effort needed. It *is worth it!* Everything that is required from us during the working-through process will be given back to us in the sheer joy and total freedom that recovery brings. It is not just freedom from our anxiety disorder, it is also the freedom to be ourselves, not who we think we should be.

The working-through process is similar for everyone. The only difference is our personal stress threshold. Some people may have reached the point where they cannot tolerate even the smallest stress.

Other people may have a higher threshold of stress. The time it takes people to recover will vary. The individual stress threshold plays a part, but the amount of effort and discipline we put into our recovery is most important.

The first attack is usually a result of either a build-up of stress or a major life stress. In other words, the anxiety and/or attack happened when we reached the limit of our individual threshold of stress. This doesn't mean we are weak. It simply means we have reached our stress limit, just as most people will reach their stress limit at some point in their life. Continual worry about the symptoms of anxiety and attacks only increases our stress and lowers our threshold.

As I said in Chapter 1, it is not so much the external stress that creates our difficulties. It is the way we perceive and deal with them that creates the problems. We deal with stress by trying to be who we think we should be. We turn off any emotions we have, such as anger or grief, and take care of everyone else. So many people have commented to me that, in times of major stress, they were fine. They were able to look after everyone else and do everything that needed to be done, and they can't understand why they are now having problems. And that is the problem. They were not taking care of themselves!

As we begin the working-through process it is helpful if we understand how low our stress threshold is and how high our anxiety is. Using the scale in Figure 10.1 will help us to estimate our levels.

If our stress threshold is extremely low we may not be able to tolerate even the smallest daily stress. Our stress threshold would be

Figure 10.1

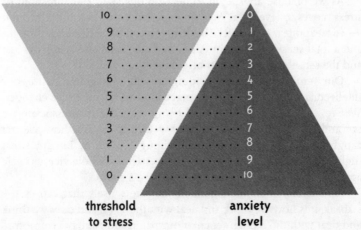

threshold   anxiety
to stress   level

zero while our anxiety level would be ten. At level five we are able to tolerate the daily stress/es, but will find our anxiety level rising if there is a break in our normal daily routine. At level ten we are able to deal with almost any stress without becoming anxious. The working-through process means working to bring our threshold to stress back to normal levels while decreasing our anxiety level.

It's no use just hearing or reading about panic anxiety management skills. We have to practise them. There will be occasions when we say we're not getting any better, nothing has changed. If we are not getting results it usually means we are not practising enough, or even not practising at all!

Understanding setbacks

Setbacks are unavoidable. In fact, the more we have the better! Each setback teaches us more about ourselves and our disorder. They challenge us to strengthen and refine our cognitive skills, and to bring our emotional development in line with our intellectual development.

To work through to recovery we need to understand why setbacks happen. As an example, our threshold of stress may now be at level zero. At the lower threshold levels, we get caught up time and again in our panic and our anxiety-producing thoughts and symptoms. When we begin the process of recovery we need to meditate every day, to become mindful and learn to control our thoughts. This is what is important at these levels—learning to manage and control our disorder.

As we practise and begin to develop our skills our threshold of stress moves to level one. We then experience our first breakthrough —we feel no fear or anxiety. This brings a complete clarity of thought and a total sense of freedom. All fear of our panic and anxiety is lost and the sense of freedom can be exhilarating.

Our emotional understanding briefly integrates with our intellectual understanding. Our perception of our disorder changes. We see, emotionally, how it is all being created. If we dissociate we see and understand emotionally how it happens and how we get caught up in our panic and anxiety thoughts about it. But any stress higher than level one will be enough to start the whole vicious cycle again. Inevitably, this happens and we have a setback.

Remember, it is not so much the stress itself that causes the setback. It is how we think and deal with the stress and how we think and deal with the reemergence of our panic and anxiety symptoms.

When a stress is higher than our threshold, we automatically slip back to being 'who we think we should be' and we slip back into our anxiety disorder thinking. Anxiety and panic follow. We become so caught up in it all over again that we think the breakthrough was a fluke and that we are not going to recover.

When this happens we need to identify why we have had a setback. We need to become aware of the current stresses in our life and how we are reacting to them. Whatever the stress is, it will be higher than we can tolerate at this point. If we are working from zero tolerance to stress, identification of why we are having a setback is not difficult—normal day-to-day stress will trigger our automatic cycle of thinking and behaving.

It could be that we dissociated and had an attack and hooked into our panic and anxiety thoughts. We may have been thinking about a personal situation and how we could resolve it. We may have been thinking about how guilty we feel about something that we did or did not do or said or did not say. We may have said 'yes' to doing something when we actually wanted to say 'no'. We may have acted from the position of being who we thought we should be and, in doing so, invalidated our self in some way. There may be family problems, a difficult financial or work situation, children home on school holidays, catching a virus, being physically sick. Any of these and more can trigger our panic and anxiety-producing thoughts.

If we are not sure why we are having a setback, we can write a list of everything that is currently happening in our life. To complete the list, we can write down how many times we have taken time out to meditate or practise some other form of relaxation. Then estimate how much time we have put into working with our thinking. That usually gives us the complete answer as to why we are experiencing a setback.

When we become aware of why it has happened, the next step is to resolve any issues relating to the stress, and to let the setback happen without buying into thoughts that we will never recover, that we are hopeless and a failure. Our threshold of stress will continue to rise as long as we continue with our management skills. We then reach level two. Our emotional understanding again integrates with our intellectual understanding and the sense of clarity and freedom reappears. But any stress higher than level two will trigger a setback. Again we go through the process outlined above. This is when we need to have patience. This is the working-through process.

STEPS IN THE WORKING-THROUGH PROCESS

- Isolate the stress/es.
- Be aware of how we are thinking about them.
- Resolve any issues relating to the stress.
- Let go of anxiety-producing thoughts.
- Let the setback happen.
- Continue with meditation.
- Continue to work with our thinking.

If we are working from level zero, the first breakthrough usually lasts only for about an hour as the daily stress will again trigger our automatic way of thinking. With continued practice of the working-through process, our threshold of stress will continue to rise. We will begin to experience days and then weeks of clarity and freedom. When we have a setback after a period of freedom, everything seems much worse and more hopeless. It isn't. It is only the contrast between these two ways of being that makes it appear so. As long as we keep practising and working with it, we will ultimately be free of fears and of our disorder.

CASE HISTORIES

Betty

Betty had worked extremely hard on her recovery. She had been able to return to work three months ago and was really happy to be back in the workforce. Although she'd had the occasional bad day, Betty was able to work through them and she had begun to feel that she had finally recovered. That was until last week. Now Betty was beginning to think the disorder was returning. Her anxiety was increasing and the attacks had returned. She knew that returning to work had been stressful, but she was happy in her job. She couldn't understand why the anxiety and the attacks were back. To all intents and purposes life was normal. Her husband and children were fine. Although Betty realised it was hard to run a household and work at the same time, she felt it was worth the extra effort. Her father's death two months ago had been traumatic but she felt that couldn't be the reason. Betty wondered if it was the argument she had had with her mother and sisters. The issues had still not been resolved and each time they were together the atmosphere was quite tense. She knew the anxiety and the attacks were making her feel tense, but she couldn't understand why they had come back. Betty thought that she needed to be more aware of what was causing stress in her life.

David

David had been making little progress with his recovery and was becoming disillusioned with the recovery program. He was having difficulty finding any time for himself to concentrate on his recovery. There were so many other things that needed to be done first. He had volunteered to take on extra duties at work because of staff shortages. That meant he wasn't getting home until 7 p.m. Working late meant he spent less time with his children, so he did his best to make up for it on weekends. This interfered with the work he did for two service clubs in his area but he tried to juggle his time. This in turn was complicated by the fact that his neighbours and friends were always dropping by with requests for favours or help. On top of all this he had to stop and take time out when the anxiety and the attacks became too much. Having to find time to work on his recovery was the final straw. David was feeling quite resentful because he thought there should be some sort of recovery program that took all these demands on his time into account.

Acceptance

Our levels of acceptance for our disorder fluctuate during the working-through process. As we experience a setback we get caught up in our old ways of thinking and feeling. Some people will again doubt that they even have the disorder, and will worry that the diagnosis may be incorrect.

Non-acceptance means we are only making the situation worse for ourselves. We all have periods of doubt about the diagnosis. If this does happen it is important to go back and discuss this with our doctor.

Compounding this doubt are the anxiety and attack symptoms and how they swap and change. As soon as we get on top of one symptom, another takes its place. Any new symptom needs to be checked by our doctor and sometimes we may feel like a hypochondriac. However, it is more important for us to know what the new symptoms are instead of continually worrying. If we are told the new symptom is another anxiety symptom we need to accept the diagnosis and not get caught in the vicious circle again.

Taking care of ourselves

A proper diet and enough sleep are also very important in helping to raise our threshold of stress. If we have eating problems, it is important we seek advice to help reestablish normal eating patterns. If we are having difficulty sleeping, we can use our meditation technique to assist us in going to sleep at night or going back to sleep if we have woken with an attack. Instead of actually meditating, we simply let meditation take us into sleep.

Exercise also plays an important part in the recovery process and it is to our benefit to establish a regular exercise program. Although many of us feel totally exhausted as a result of our ongoing struggle with panic and anxiety, exercise helps us to break through this fatigue. This sounds like a contradiction, but in reality it isn't. The more exercise we take the less fatigue we will feel.

Relearning

The working-through process also involves relearning what it is like to be 'normal'. We lose sight of what it is like to be 'normal', and it is not unusual for people to interpret 'normalcy' as a setback! It isn't—we just have to relearn.

This means relearning to have a 'normal' bad day without reacting with fear that 'it is all coming back'. Returning to 'normal' means that we will have bad days just like everyone else.

We will probably have days when we feel unwell. It doesn't mean a return of the disorder—it means we are feeling unwell. We need to make sure we are eating properly and getting enough sleep. If not, we will feel tired and irritable just like everyone does when they neglect themselves. Recovery is a learning process, learning to manage and control our anxiety disorder and learning about ourselves.

CBT revisited

The question sometimes arises about how much we need to practise a CBT program to reduce our avoidance behaviour. Having to confront situations and places that we have avoided does initially place us under more stress. We need to learn to walk a fine line. There are going to be times when we feel we want to give up and we begin to despair of ever recovering. There may be times when we're feeling this way, but continually push ourselves without being aware of how much more anxiety is being generated. Then we do give up through exhaustion and despair.

Working with our avoidance behaviour and the whole process of recovery means we need to learn to care for ourselves. We need to learn when it is appropriate to pull back and take a break, as long as the break doesn't go on for weeks. After the break, begin again.

Begin again. These two words can mean so much in the working-through process. If we feel that we are not making progress, if we feel that some of our attempts didn't quite work out the way we would have liked, let them go and *begin again*.

MAKING ALLOWANCES

Making allowances for ourselves as we begin a graded exposure program is being kind to our self. We need to realise in the beginning that our cognitive skills are still rudimentary and that we must give ourselves time to develop them.

If part of our exposure program means going to dinner or the theatre, we can ask to be seated by an aisle or an exit, or both. Not so much for a quick getaway, but to help break down the feeling of being trapped. The aisle or exit is there if we do need to leave quickly. If we work with our thinking and let the anxiety and attack happen, we will find we won't need to.

Another allowance is breaking down the time we know we will have to spend in any given situation. It may be a business meeting, it may be an evening with friends, it may be doing the shopping. It could be anything.

If we know something will take two hours, work with the first hour first. Don't even think about the second hour. If the situation is too difficult and our anxiety level doesn't settle down, we can leave after the first hour. Usually, by the second hour we are not even aware the first hour is over, because we have become involved with what we are doing instead of with the anxiety and attacks.

Part of our CBT program may be doing the shopping alone. This can be broken down into easier steps. To begin with, we can go to the shop early in the morning. We will feel more comfortable about letting the anxiety and attack happen if the shop is not too crowded. As we become more confident about letting it happen, we can begin to shop at different times of the day.

Making allowances is not giving in, it is working with the disorder. Doing nothing is giving in. In the early stages of recovery, making allowances helps us to reduce the amount of pressure we feel. Making allowances indefinitely means we are not putting ourselves under enough pressure!

In the beginning there may be times when we feel we have to leave a situation. If it becomes too difficult to manage, then leave, not with a sense of failure, but accepting that this time it was too difficult. A sense of failure defeats us, not only in the short term but also in the long term. Accept the situation and let go of the worrying. There will be other times when we will be able to do it as long as we keep practising.

Psychotherapy revisited

People have asked what to do with their thoughts while working through issues in psychotherapy. There will be issues that need to be thought through and worked with, and they may also cause anxiety and attacks. If this does happen, it is very important to discuss it with our therapist so they can assist us in modifying our cognitive skills to suit our needs and the needs of therapy.

Motivation

Another important point is our motivation. If it has dropped we need to look at why. A drop in motivation also means a drop in the will-to-power. Sometimes our lack of motivation can be caused by fears of change and of growth.

The working-through process means we are getting in touch with ourselves for the first time. We become aware of how we think and react on a day-to-day basis, which usually gives us insights into ourselves we have not had before. Sometimes these insights can be quite threatening as they could signal the need for changes in our life.

A drop in motivation may mean we are avoiding these insights. Everyone wants to recover but many of us want recovery to mean we will return to our former self. This doesn't happen, as I discussed in Chapter 5.

The working-through process means we are getting in touch with ourselves, with feelings, needs and desires we may never have known existed. These will need to be integrated and their integration will mean not a return to the old, but the birth of the new.

CHAPTER 11

THE PATH TO FREEDOM

At the beginning of the working-through process, our time and energy needs to be focused on being aware of how our thoughts are creating our fear, anxiety and panic. We also need to focus on learning how to control our thinking. If we dissociate, we need to be aware of how we are inducing these states and how we hook into our thoughts and fears of them.

Responsibility

As our threshold to stress moves of higher levels, we begin to see how our need to be 'all things to all people' impacts on our overall levels of anxiety. When we are not respecting our needs, when we are not being responsible for ourselves, our anxiety and sometimes panic will let us know in no uncertain terms!

As we move into this stage of recovery we will feel the stark contrast between the periods of freedom and clarity and the periods when we become caught up again in our anxiety and panic. During the recovery process we will continually move between these two ways of being. The more we take responsibility for ourselves, the more we integrate the emotional with the intellectual, the more the freedom and clarity becomes a permanent part of our lives.

Taking responsibility for ourselves can be frightening because it challenges all our core beliefs of who we think we should be. As we become more mindful we see how we are not being honest with ourselves nor responsible for ourselves. We will see how we disrespect ourselves, time and time again, by being who we think we should be. We will see how we 'turn off' our emotions and how we negate our own needs.

This creates so much of our underlying anxiety. Yet, even if we honour the responsibility to our self, if we express our emotions, meet our own needs, we can still feel anxious. It appears as if we are caught in another trap. We are not.

Anxiety drivers

There are actually a number of different types of anxiety and during the recovery process we need to learn to distinguish between them. Although they have the same symptoms, the 'driver' of the anxiety can differ from our basic panic and anxiety thinking.

When we begin to become aware of our own needs and feel our own emotions, we immediately think we are 'bad' or selfish. As a client said to me, 'We have been taught to believe that if we feel our emotions we are bad.' If we meet our own needs, we are being not only 'bad' we are being selfish as well!

This is one particular driver of our anxiety: meeting our own needs, or even thinking of meeting our own needs, feeling and expressing our emotions *versus* what we have been taught. This conflict generates anxiety and sometimes panic. Meeting our own needs, feeling and expressing our emotions appropriately, are not signs of 'bad' or selfish behaviour. They are signs of healthy emotional development.

Another driver of our anxiety is the negation and invalidation of our self in other ways. We try to be the perfect person to everyone we come into contact with. We 'wear' a number of different 'masks' depending on the situation and the person we are with. The process of recovery shows us quite clearly the choices we have in this. We can continue to be who we think we should be, with the underlying anxiety this generates, or we can begin to learn a healthier way of living our life. If we choose the latter, this brings yet another driver of our anxiety and this is growth anxiety.

Growth anxiety occurs when we begin to challenge our belief systems and begin to take what we think is the biggest risk of all— letting go of our need to be perfect and our need to liked and loved by everyone we come into contact with.

Working with growth anxiety is exactly the same as working with our other forms of anxiety. We allow it to be there and not add to it by getting caught up in our 'what if' thinking. When we can allow our growth anxiety to be there, we can begin to learn who we are.

We can take off our masks, begin to know and meet our own needs, feel our full range of emotions. In doing so we take responsibility for ourselves and our mental health.

Growth anxiety heralds change and the *fear of change* is yet another driver of our anxiety. We need to realise that there have been other times in our life when we have made major changes. We may have felt this fear when we initially began working, when we went to university, got married or had children. That fear is the same as we are feeling now. If we can remember those other occasions we will see this fear is not unique. We have felt it before. Back then, we went ahead and did what we needed to do, even though we were feeling unsure and feeling the fear. And we need to do this again—allow the anxiety to be there without hooking into panic and anxiety thoughts, and allow ourselves to do what we need to do for us and our mental health!

A time of learning

With each step of working through we gain new awareness, new knowledge and increased strength. The process does become easier and more tolerable. This is life, this is growth. It is a continual evolving process. At times we will feel tired, defenceless and vulnerable. If we don't hook into our panic anxiety thoughts about this, the feelings don't last. We will begin to know and understand why we are feeling this way. We will get to know quite a lot about our self. In fact, sometimes we will wish we didn't know so much!

It is a time of learning to trust ourselves and this includes allowing ourselves to make mistakes. Mistakes can actually become our teachers, along with our anxiety and panic, if we are willing to learn from them.

We will become aware that we do have a choice in everything we think and everything we do. At each step we can take what we need and let go of what we need to. At some points in the recovery process, it may mean rearranging things to make life a little more comfortable and a little bit easier while the emotional and intellectual integration is worked through. We can choose to set limits if we need to. We can choose to move at our own pace. It is going to feel unfamiliar, we will feel vulnerable and the fear will be there, but so too is our self's determination to grow.

Anxiety disorders are destructive. They tear away the very fabric of our whole being. They destroy our way of life. The attacks and the anxiety terrify us sometimes to the extent that normal everyday living is non-existent. Yet we do not recognise in this destruction an equally positive force. The destruction can be a positive turning point in becoming our real self.

CASE HISTORIES

Jane

It was one of those beautiful autumn evenings. The light from the setting sun filtered through the trees and their leaves blazed with colour. Jane wondered how many other people were looking at this natural masterpiece as they hurried home after the day's work. Jane knew that she had never taken much notice before. Now was different. Once or twice a day she would be struck by the beauty of her surroundings, a moment here, a moment there. But those moments were precious in their spontaneity. They added to the peace she felt within herself. She was amazed at the last few years of her life. It had not always been like this. The years of panic disorder/agoraphobia had appeared to take everything from her. They were desolate years. The fight back was long and hard but she knew now it had been worth it. Everything that had been taken away from her had been given back a thousand-fold. She was at peace with herself and she was free.

Peter

Peter was exhilarated. It was early morning and he had reached halfway in a 10 km bike ride along the coast road. He wished he had brought his camera. Peter had loved photography ever since he was a child. He had always wanted to be a photographer, and now he was one. He thought of his parents. They had both worked long and hard to pay for his university fees, and they were proud of him when he received his PhD and entered the world of academia. Panic disorder/agoraphobia had changed all that. As Peter progressed towards recovery he realised that academic life was not for him. He struggled silently with the realisation for three years because he didn't want to let his parents down. He even studied for another degree, hoping to combat his disquiet. It didn't work, and he made the break to follow his dream of being a photographer. He knew he was taking a risk but he also knew it was worth it. He was free.

The ultimate answer and the ultimate resources are within us. It can sometimes hurt and it can sometimes be frightening. It can mean different things for all of us but ultimately we hold the path to freedom within our self.

The path to freedom

What does fear hold us back from? From ourselves. From being free. Being free to be able to be all we could be. There is no exact blueprint on how to get to know our self, no external guide or map we can look at. The blueprint is our self. Mindfulness can become our guide and it will show us how to work through the stages of the process. From the first step to the last, it will be an individual journey. But what a journey!

Being afraid is all right. Being hesitant is all right. Feeling vulnerable and defenceless is all right. They are all part of the ongoing development of our self. When we begin to work with it, we won't know where we are, where we are going or what will happen to us along the way. This is all right too.

As we let the process continue our trust in our self and the process grows. We begin to see familiar landmarks and the bridges we need to cross. We get to know the rest stops on the way and we know with growing certainty that we are headed in the right direction.

It does mean changes, but all the resources necessary will be found within us and we will find them waiting for us at each step. Not only will we find them waiting, we will find they have been there all along. There will be times of uncertainty when we turn back or stop along the way. When we are ready to begin again, we will find the resources are still there within us.

All the energy that we have used to suppress our self can be freed for us to use in whatever way we wish. It is a gift of recovery which is waiting for all of us. The time will come again for change, far less dramatically, but come again it will and there will be new challenges to meet. This call for growth is part of the evolutionary development in all of us.

It is a question of how honest we are being with ourselves, but this honesty is the way of self-determination, of being all we could be.

It is our choice.

BIBLIOGRAPHY

American Psychiatric Association 1980, *Diagnostic & Statistical Manual of Mental Disorders*, 3rd edn, APA: Washington.

American Psychiatric Association 1990, *Information Booklet on Anxiety Disorders*, Commission of Public Affairs and the Division of Public Affairs of the American Psychiatrists Association, APA: Washington.

American Psychiatric Association 1994, *Diagnostic & Statistical Manual of Mental Disorders*, 4th edn, APA: Washington.

Andrews G, Peters L, & Teesson M. 1994, *The Measurement of Consumer Outcomes in Mental Health*, Australian Health Ministers Advisory Council, Australian Govt Publishing Service: Canberra.

Argyle N & Roth M. 1990, 'The phenomenological study of 90 patients with panic disorder', *Psychiatric Developments*, 7,187–209 cited in Argyle N, Solyom C & Solyom L. 1991, 'The structure of phobias in panic disorder', *British Journal of Psychiatry*, 159, 378–82.

Arthur-Jones J & Fox B. 1994, *Cross-cultural Comparisons of Panic Disorder*, Panic Anxiety Hub: Goolwa SA.

Australian Bureau of Statistics 1997 'Mental Health and Wellbeing: Profile of Adults', ABS Catalogue No. 4326.0: Canberra.

Benson H. 1975, *The Relaxation Response*, William Morrow: New York.

Boyd JH & Crump T. 1991, 'Westphal's Agoraphobia', *Journal of Anxiety Disorders* 5, 77–86.

British Medical Journal 1998. Editorial. 'Antidepressant discontinuation reactions', 316,1105–6.

Brown GW & Harris TO. 1993, 'Aetiology of anxiety and depressive disorders in an inner-city population. 1. Early adversity', *Psychological Medicine*, 23, 143–54.

Brayley J, Bradshaw G & Pols R. 1991, *Guidelines for the Prevention and Management of Benzodiazepine Dependence*, AGPS: Canberra.

Brunton P. 1965, *The Quest of the Overself*, Samuel Weiser Inc: York Beach, Maine.

Commission of Public Affairs and the Division of Public Affairs of the American Psychiatrists Association 1990, *Information Booklet on Anxiety Disorders*, APA: Washington.

Cox BJ, Norton GR, Swinson RP & Endler NS. 1990, 'Substance abuse and panic-related anxiety, a critical review', *Behavior Research and Therapy* 28 (5): 385–93.

Evans L. 1995, *A Follow-up of an Agoraphobia Treatment Program*, Commonwealth Dept of Human Services and Health: Canberra.

Fewtrell WD & O'Connor KP. 1988, 'Dizziness and depersonalisation', *Advanced Behaviour Research and Therapy*, 10: 201–18.

Greenberg P. et al. 1999, 'The economic burden of anxiety disorders in the 1990s', *Journal of Clinical Psychiatry*, 60(7): 427–35.

Hafner J. 1986, *Marriage and Mental Illness*, Guilford Press: New York.

Hafner J, Arthur-Jones J & Viner R. 1996, *Evaluation of the Effectiveness of Consumer Driven Panic Anxiety-management Workshops*. Anxiety Disorders Consumer Support & Prevention Project no 26003, Dept of Health and Family Services: Canberra, ACT.

Kabat-Zinn J, Massion A, Kristeller J, Peterson LG, Fletcher KE, Pbert L., Lenderking L. & Santorelli SF. 1992, 'Effectiveness of a meditation-based stress reduction program in the treatment of anxiety disorders', *American Journal of Psychiatry*, 149(7): 936–43.

Kenardy J, Oei TPS, Ryan P, & *Evans L. 1988, 'Attribution of panic attacks: patient perspective', *Journal of Anxiety Disorders*, 2: 243–51.

Knott VJ, 1990, 'Neuroelectrical activity related to panic disorder', *Progress in Neuropsychopharmacology and Biological Psychiatry* 14: 697–707, cited in McNally RJ. 1994, *Panic Disorder: A Critical Analysis*, The Guilford Press: New York.

Malison RT & Price LH. 1990, 'Panic states', *Current Opinions In Psychiatry* 3: 229–34.

Oswald I. 1962, *Sleeping and Waking: Physiology & Psychology*, Elsevier Publishing Company: Amsterdam.

Otto MW, Gould RA, & Pollack MH. 1994, 'Cognitive-behavioural treatment of panic disorder: considerations for the treatment of patients over the long term', *Psychiatiric Annals*, 24(6).

Phobic Trust of New Zealand 1991, *Phobos* 5(7).

Putman FW. 1989, *Diagnosis and Treatment of Multiple Personality Disorder*, Guildford Press: New York.

South Australian Health Commission 1998, *Anxiety Disorders Review*, Lewkowicz G, South Australian Department of Human Services and Health: Adelaide.

Sheehan D 1983, *The Anxiety Disease*, Charles Scribner's Sons: New York.

Sheehan D, Ballenger J & Jacobsen G. 1980, 'Treatment of endogenous anxiety with phobic, hysterical and hypochondrical symptoms', *Archives of General Psychiatry* 37: 51–9, cited in Siegel L, Jones W & Wilson J. 1990, 'Economic and life consequences experienced by a group of individuals with panic disorder', *Journal of Anxiety Disorders* 4: 201–11.

Tart CT. 1972, *Altered States of Consciousness*, Doubleday Anchor: New York.

Task Force on Meditation 1977, 'Position statement on meditation', *American Journal of Psychiatry* 134: 720, cited in Kutz et al. 1985, 'Dynamic psychotherapy, the relaxation response and mindfulness meditation', *American Journal of Psychiatry* 142: 1–7.

Trungpa C. 1986, *Shambhala—The Sacred Path of the Warrior*, Bantam Books: New York.

Uhde TW. 1994, *Principles and Practice of Sleep Medicine*, 2nd edition, Chap. 84, WB Saunders & Co.: Philadelphia.

Weekes C. 1992, *Self Help for your Nerves*, 28th edn, Angus & Robertson: Sydney.

7/02